Contents

This book is dedicated to my wife, Margaret.

Planning, Teaching and Class Management in Primary Schools

Meeting the Standards

Denis Hayes

David Fulton Publishers
London

David Fulton Publishers Ltd
Ormond House, 26–27 Boswell Street, London WC1N 3JD

First published in Great Britain by David Fulton Publishers 1999

Note: The right of Denis Hayes to be identified as author of this work has been asserted by him in accordance with the Copyright, Designs and Patents Act 1988.

Copyright © Denis Hayes 1999

British Library Cataloguing in Publication Data
A catalogue record for this book is available from the British Library

ISBN 1–85346–610–7

Typeset by Helen Skelton, London
Printed in Great Britain by The Cromwell Press, Trowbridge, Wilts.

Preface

Learning to teach is exciting and challenging. Despite conflicting claims about effective policy, standards, parental rights, societal obligations and political aspirations, it is still the relationship between teacher and taught, the joy of discovering new things and the thrill of achievement which lie at the heart of education. And regardless of the changes to the curriculum that have taken place over the years, the ability to plan, teach and manage children to give them the best possible chance of learning remains an essential element of the teacher's role.

It is sometimes difficult for inexperienced teachers and trainees to realise that previous status and hard-won accolades count for little when they meet a new group of children. Most pupils take only a passing interest in a teacher's past successes or failures; they are principally interested in finding answers to some key questions:

- Can this person teach?
- Can this person keep order?
- Is this person nice or nasty?
- Will this person be interesting and fun to be with?
- Can I trust this person?
- Is this person for me or against me?

Pupils may not express their thoughts in quite this way, of course, but they will quickly discover the answers to their unspoken questions through a variety of strategies which children have used down the years to test out new teachers, including calling out, innocent questions, sighs and depressed looks and feigned ignorance. Every teacher must be ready to counteract all such ploys by positive means, notably through careful lesson planning, enthusiastic teaching and a no-nonsense attitude. Perseverance, a willingness to learn from mistakes and determination are essential attributes for every aspiring teacher.

In addition, all novice teachers discover that what appears to come so easily to the experienced teacher is, in fact, extremely demanding and difficult to achieve and sustain ...

- The class teacher calls for quiet and the children stop talking. The student teacher does the same thing and some children stop, while others continue. As the student is busy admonishing the disobedient ones, those who stopped talking re-commence their conversations.
- The class teacher prepares a worksheet for the lesson in a few minutes. The student attempts something similar and is up until late at night.
- The class teacher chats to parents at the door in a relaxed and personable way. The student tries to do the same and gets her words tangled.
- The class teacher marks some books and finishes them in half an hour, together with some helpful comments at the end of the page. The student takes three times as long and agonises over what to write.

These examples are not given to depress trainees but to reinforce the often-overlooked axiom that teaching does not 'come naturally' to the majority of people. There are some students who seem to have an indefinable instinct for the job, but most have to battle and persevere with the challenges which inevitably arise in a situation where one adult has responsibility for the education of large numbers of pupils. All those who enter upon teaching must expect some hard times before reaping the rich rewards of a fulfilling career.

Denis Hayes
Exmouth, November 1998

Introduction

The standards

Planning, Teaching and Class Management in Primary Schools is intended to help students and those in their first year of teaching develop expertise in planning, teaching and class management. As the advice offered in the book is considered, weighed and incorporated into classroom life, it will help students to gain their qualified teacher status (QTS) and encourage new teachers to develop skills, attitudes and understanding of the job which will not only allow them to meet successfully the necessary requirements for good teaching, but to exceed them.

In order to achieve the required standards for QTS, the government insists that student teachers demonstrate that they have achieved competence in a number of closely defined areas as set out in Circular 10/97 (DfEE 1997) and Circular 4/98 (DfEE 1998) relating to core subjects, information and communication technology, and planning, teaching and class management. In addition, all new teachers in their first year of teaching have successfully to complete a probationary (induction) year in which they must demonstrate that they have built upon the expertise gained through their initial training (DfEE 1998). This book deals largely with the standards covering planning, teaching and class management, including some important information on issues relating to assessment, recording and reporting.

You may feel a little intimidated when you first read the many demands made by the statements. If so, remember that if your lessons are appropriately planned with reference to the National Curriculum and the school's schemes of work, children are learning enthusiastically, and you are controlling the class and assessing their progress consistently, then you are doing an effective job. In practice, teachers, mentors and tutors have to interpret the standards flexibly or few students would ever successfully complete their training, as there is hardly a qualified teacher in the land who would match the standards in every detail at all times and in all circumstances. If you are a student teacher, those responsible for assessing your progress know that the statements provide a framework against which to monitor progress, but they are not so foolish as to imagine that the route to competence requires perfection in everything! It would be wholly unnecessary and counterproductive to go through each standard in turn in the hope of finding one small area in your repertoire that was less than perfect.

Nevertheless, reaching and maintaining high standards requires a lot of hard work and perseverance. The contents of *Planning, Teaching and Class Management in Primary Schools* will make this demanding task easier as you reflect upon the advice and suggestions provided under each heading.

It is also important to remember that although the term 'standards' is used in DfEE documentation, the requirements are expressed as a series of statements about the way in which an ideal teacher would perform in an ideal school under ideal conditions. Like every other set of end-point statements, they have to be interpreted in context. Some school situations are much more demanding for teachers and students than others. Some teachers are more supportive and supported than their colleagues. Mentors vary in their proficiency. Classes contain children with variable attitudes to learning, quality of resources and levels of equipment. No school is ideal, so you simply have to buckle down and persevere with what you have got.

Finally, to gain newly qualified teacher (NQT) status, trainee teachers must demonstrate, when assessed, that they have met each of the standards for every subject that they have been trained to teach. However, although every standard has to be satisfactorily achieved, there will always be some areas of competence which are stronger than others.

In non-core, non-specialist subjects, students must meet the required standards but with the support, if necessary, of a teacher experienced in the subject concerned. The statements therefore apply most immediately to core subjects and the specialist subject.

NQTs have a profile of their work in the form of a career entry profile to use as a basis for their further professional development in which strengths and weaknesses are specified. As they progress through their careers, headteachers and senior staff are expected to give them support in enhancing the weaker areas and becoming more expert in the stronger ones. You only have to be 'good enough' to gain QTS, not perfect. Learning how to improve your effectiveness as a teacher goes on throughout your professional career

Using this book

Planning, Teaching and Class Management in Primary Schools provides a blend of practical ideas and suggestions, presented in a form to help you improve your practical classroom teaching or for discussion in seminars and workshops. There are statements which relate specifically to planning (P), teaching lessons (TA and

TMS), special educational needs (SEN), assessment of pupils' progress (A), reporting to parents (R) and critical reflection (CR). Although aspects of staff membership and related responsibilities are only dealt with briefly, fuller details may be obtained from *Professional Issues for Teachers and Student Teachers* (1999) edited by Mike Cole.

The following details should also be noted:

- the wording of some standards statements has been modified, especially where statements have been considered together – for the exact wording, consult the Circular;
- the section number from Circular 4/98 is placed in brackets at the head of each section (e.g. Section B, 4e);
- each standard (or, in a small number of cases, group of standards) is assigned its own set of comments under subheadings with a 'keynote' statement for each;
- a short 'competence check' is provided at the end of each section for students, tutors and mentors to use as a basis for discussion and evaluation;
- cross references to related sections within the book will refer to their code numbers (e.g. TA3);
- cross references with the book *Foundations of Primary Teaching* (Hayes 1996) will carry the initials FPT and a chapter number.

The standards statements contained in Circulars 10/97 and 4/98 which form the substance of this book can be used in a number of different ways (see Table 1). It is important to reinforce the fact that however rigid the standards statements appear to be, they should be treated as beacons to guide your path rather than forest fires to scorch and hinder.

Table 1   Ways of using the standards statements

- As a basis for planning and curriculum continuity and development
- To write reflective commentaries or journals on the issues raised through the statements
- For students and tutors/mentors to agree a specific focus during classroom observation
- As a basis for a final assessment of student competence in planning, teaching and class management
- As a framework for mentor training

Chapter 1

Planning (P1–9)

Planning your lessons requires competence in nine key areas:

P1 What is taught.
P2 What teaching and assessment strategies are employed.
P3 What tasks are set to challenge and motivate pupils.
P4 How pupils' targets are set.
P5 How pupils with learning difficulties are dealt with.
P6 How lessons are structured.
P7 How continuity is provided between lessons.
P8 How a lesson incorporates the affective domain.
P9 How a lesson conforms to the National Curriculum programme.

P1 Identify clear and appropriate teaching objectives and content

(Section B, 4a, i; see FPT, Chapter 5)

What you need to take account of to meet this standard ...

Terminology needs clarifying

Words such as 'aim', 'goal', 'objective', 'purpose' and 'intention' are liberally scattered throughout the language and mean different things to different teachers. Most commonly, the words 'aim' and 'goal' are concerned with final outcomes. The word 'objective' is most often used to describe the steps on the way to achieving the aim. For example, in learning to use a protractor, objectives may include an understanding about direction, the ability to employ appropriate terminology, an understanding of angular measurement, identifying, constructing and measuring angles using crude instruments, before finally using different types of protractor in problem-solving or investigations. The words 'purpose' and 'intention' are used interchangeably as broad terms describing what a teacher hopes to achieve in the lesson. It is worth clarifying what you mean when you use terms and ensure that the person reading your lesson plan shares that view. In reality, pupils who appear to have succeeded in achieving the aim (target) on one occasion may still have only a tentative grasp of the subject area and require regular reminders and opportunity to rehearse and practise their skills.

Keynote: To use planning terminology consistently.

The main lesson purpose

If the lesson is without purpose it is probably not worth teaching. You should be clear about whether the principal purpose is to extend pupils' knowledge, develop their conceptual understanding, practise skills or consolidate former learning. Even if it is a combination of some or all of these elements, it is worth clarifying this in your lesson plan by stating the intentions under the three headings: knowledge; concepts; skills. In broad terms, most of the knowledge will be provided by you through direct teaching or pupils finding out for themselves from books and databases. Most of the concepts will be developed through conversation, question-and-answer sessions and investigative play. Skills enhancement may take the form of consolidating knowledge and concepts through problem solving or improving ability through application to specific practical tasks.

Keynote: To be clear about the lesson purpose.

The likely learning patterns

In lesson preparation it is important to be clear not only about its purpose but about the way in which the purpose is to be realised. Some forms of learning can be mastered by means of following a number of well-defined consecutive stages (such as using computer software); some learning takes place by means of overlapping stages in which a presentation of new ideas is necessarily preceded by reviewing earlier ones (such as in a science investigation); some forms of learning are more random and do not follow an obvious pattern (such as a problem-solving activity which can take one of many possible directions). Many lessons take the form of an initial teacher introduction, followed by set tasks and a conclusion, though note that if your introduction is only used to explain the tasks without improving pupils' understanding or sharpening their appetite for discovering more, an important opportunity for learning has been lost.

Keynote: To think about the way in which pupils learn best.

Mismatches between teaching objectives and learning outcomes

Lessons should be planned in such a way that the teaching approach helps to bring about particular learning outcomes. However, teachers cannot legislate for what children will learn and it is sometimes different from their original intentions. Sometimes, lessons take unexpected turns and the anticipated learning outcomes are not achieved. This can happen for many reasons, such as an interesting diversion due to a pupil's discovery, the posing of a thoughtful question or the re-interpretation of a task that provides for an exciting appraisal of existing methods. If the lesson involves a lot of direct-transmission teaching in which the teacher dominates the talk, the outcome is more predictable. If the lesson involves a lot of interaction between teacher and taught, especially if pupils are being encouraged to ask questions and pose problems, it is sometimes more difficult to predict outcomes, as conversations may take unexpected directions. Due to the unpredictable nature of learning, it is important to spend some part of each lesson assessing (through what pupils say, write or do) the extent to which your teaching objectives have been matched by pupils' learning (see A1).

Keynote: To take account of the way in which teaching intentions may have to be modified.

Teaching about learning

There are occasions when the lesson content is less important than the process of learning. For instance, pupils may be involved in collaborative ventures or discussions where the purpose is primarily concerned with the development of social and interactive skills. Although the National Curriculum requires that pupils acquire specific skills and concepts, there are many occasions (such as structured play activities) when 'learning about learning' through social interaction is essential. Similarly, it is important for children to learn how to work independently without relying too much on their peers or an adult. Some children take time to gain the necessary skills and confidence to make their own decisions; others find it hard to take anybody else's opinions into account! You have to decide how much time to devote to activities which enhance the pupils' abilities in collaborative and independent learning modes. It is rare that these can be accomplished in a hurry; nevertheless, part of your job is to help children to help themselves (see TMS9).

Keynote: To ensure that pupils have the necessary study skills to complete tasks successfully.

Differences between original intentions and final outcomes should be exploited.

Competence check

☐ I am clear about the main purpose of the lesson
☐ I have thought through the likely patterns of learning
☐ I have taken account of other learning that might take place

P2 Specify the teaching approaches and assessment strategies for achieving stated objectives

(Section B, 4a, i)

What you need to take account of to meet this standard ...

Your intentions and children's capability

All teaching approaches must bear in mind what you want the children to learn and the abilities, speed of work and motivation of the children in the class. Planning lessons and taking account of teaching approaches needs to be guided by what pupils have achieved and are capable of achieving with your help. It is important to know what children already understand and what they have already experienced. Lessons cannot normally be planned in isolation from the classroom context in which they are to be taught if they are to be effective. If your lesson plans assume too little of pupils, they will become bored and restless; if they assume too much, you will spend most of the lesson reinforcing previous lessons which were never properly mastered.

Keynote: To know how far pupils have progressed.

There is no such thing as a single teaching approach

Different lessons require different approaches and assessment strategies. It is unwise to adopt a single approach – such as transmission teaching where you do most of the talking or group work in which you do little more than monitor progress – and claim that it 'works for me'. It is probable that your preferred approach is more appropriate to some circumstances than to others. For example, you may want to spend more time on explanation at the start of a new phase of learning than you do when pupils have grasped the basic principles and are spending time practising what they have been taught. If you are obliged to incorporate the class teacher's approach into your teaching, work hard to make a success of it, but discuss the possibility of adopting different approaches from time to time. It is important to visit other classes to widen your experience and see the variety of methods used.

Keynote: To utilise a range of teaching approaches appropriate to the situation.

Greater differentiation requires more involved preparation

Lessons in which every child does more or less the same work will require less differentiation and matching of task than lessons in which a range of learning needs have been catered for through different activities. However, the time required to plan, prepare and present differentiated learning tasks may be considerable. There are a number of ways of approaching the process of matching lesson content to ability (see FPT, Chapter 7). First, in the introductory phase of the lesson, you have to decide whether it is better to address the whole class at the same time about the lesson or speak to each group separately if they are doing different work. If you choose the latter, the children waiting for your attention must have a worthwhile 'holding task' until you become available. Second, the tasks must reflect the children's ability in terms of the vocabulary used, the concepts involved and the difficulty of the activity. Third, the final phase of a lesson increases in complexity in direct proportion to the range of different activities taking place. For instance, it is easier to conclude a lesson in which all the groups are dealing with computation exercises than it is if one group is doing maths, another problem solving and another art work.

Keynote: To ensure that the teaching and tasks are appropriate and manageable.

The overall teaching approach should incorporate a variety of methods

A teaching approach should be sufficiently flexible to allow for variation throughout the course of a lesson. For instance, the lesson may begin with a rehearsal of previously covered points, assessing pupils' understanding through a question-and-answer session, introducing the new material through demonstration and exposition, further question and answer to check understanding and extend pupils' thinking, allocating tasks, monitoring work on an individual or group basis, briefly reviewing the lesson with the whole class, and summarising key concepts or facilitating reporting-back from groups (see TMS5 and 6). Your own role in this unfolding lesson will depend on how much you want children to listen to you (or to one another), how much you want them to persevere with tasks and how much time you want to spend in determining what they have learned. For instance, on some occasions you will be teaching directly, on other occasions (such as hearing children's explanations about their work) you will be listening, and on others (such as when you are observing children at work without intervening) you will be assessing their understanding.

Keynote: To build a repertoire of methods.

Formative and summative assessment are both important

Assessment for every lesson should concentrate on the ongoing work as well as the anticipated end product. If you attempt to develop lessons that are too complex, you will not have the time to monitor pupils' progress and will have to rely on your summative assessments after the conclusion of the session when you mark work or check answers. Formative assessment takes place as you note children's responses, listen to their conversations, discuss their problems with them and examine their written output. It takes place before you offer advice, state an opinion about work, explain new possibilities or show that something is wrong. In order to do any of these things you have first had to monitor the situation, weigh up the possibilities and intervene as appropriate. Summative assessment has to wait until the task is completed or a natural juncture has been reached in the work whereby an evaluation of present progress can be carried out. It is important that you are clear about the school's marking policy when making a summative assessment (see FPT, Chapter 10).

Keynote: To use formative and summative assessment strategies effectively.

Assessment relies on a range of factors

Assessment should take account of the pupils' previous experience, the amount of help they received in completing the task and the level of difficulty they experienced in completing the task. You must also accept the possibility that pupils' progress has been hindered by your poor explanations, inappropriate match of task with ability, or failure to motivate and encourage their determined efforts. Where possible, involve pupils in evaluating the quality of their own work by allowing them to explain what they have done and why. Assessment is only useful if it assists the pupil's understanding, promotes a keener interest in the work and is accompanied by appropriate support in the form of advice, guidance or explanation. It is also important to take note of what pupils' achievements might tell you about your own teaching methods and effectiveness.

Keynote: To take account of all the facts before drawing conclusions.

Assessment requires careful judgement

Some assessment can be carried out through a formal test in which children write down answers to set questions; for example, during Standard Assessment Tasks (SATs) and schools' internal monitoring procedures (see A4). Your own assessment of their progress must rely more heavily upon regular inspections of their written and visual output, and verbal exchanges with them about aspects of the work, including question and answer. These two approaches (written/visual output; verbal exchanges) are less straightforward than they seem. Written outputs cannot always be taken at face value as some children find difficulty in record-ing things that they understand perfectly well. Children's answers to teachers' questions are often cloaked with embarrassment, fear about being wrong and inexperience with expressing themselves (see TA5 and TMS7). Your assessments will be more effective once you have gained the pupils' trust.

Keynote: To use the appropriate assessment technique.

It is unwise to jump to conclusions

There may be many reasons for children struggling with their work, including a lack of understanding of concepts, uncertainty about what is required, poor application to task and low motivation. Although in recent years there has been an emphasis upon monitoring work with respect to National Curriculum levels of achievement, this is only one way of judging achievement. Children may under-achieve in key subjects due to a combination of factors involving home and school, or they may achieve highly in areas which are not formally tested. Nevertheless, regardless of the particular measure you use, part of your lesson preparation should always include asking the question, 'How will I know if learning intentions have been achieved?'

Keynote: To take proper account of the factors underlying achievement.

Assessment is not a once-and-for-all event.

Competence check

- ☐ I am sufficiently clear about my teaching approach
- ☐ I have taken the pupils' differing abilities into account in my planning
- ☐ I have a clear idea about how I will assess the success of my lesson

P3 Set tasks, including homework, which challenge and motivate pupils

(Section B, 4a, ii and iii)

What you need to take account of to meet this standard ...

Challenge comes in many forms

A task may be challenging due to its conceptual difficulty, the level of skill required to carry it out or the length of time it takes to complete it. Challenging work should be invigorating and inspiring rather than disheartening and repressing. Challenges should stretch the children's thinking but not prove insurmountable. If you set homework that makes unreasonable demands upon children, it will prove to be counterproductive and may result in complaints from parents.

Keynote: To set tasks which allow all children to find success.

Homework should not be an afterthought

Lesson planning should, where possible, include some reference to homework tasks. Although some teachers simply ask children to 'finish off the work', this is not always desirable as faster workers have little to do and slower (possibly more conscientious) workers have too much to complete. Homework should help to reinforce the day's work, allow opportunity for extending the pupils' knowledge or stimulate their thinking (OFSTED 1995). It is useful to have a broad homework plan for the month ahead which can be changed if necessary but provides a structure for continuity. Note that some schools have specific homework tasks which have to be administered in much the same way as any other part of the curriculum programme. If this is the case, introduce the tasks with the same enthusiasm and vitality that you would use were they your own choice.

Keynote: To consider homework as part of lesson planning.

Homework tasks are not a substitute for active teaching

Although investigative and problem-solving homework tasks help to secure understanding, extend thinking and enhance collaboration, they should not be seen as a substitute for direct, interactive classroom teaching which emanates from your own subject knowledge and ability to convey information in a relevant, persuasive manner. Similarly, children gain the most from experiential learning (through play or exploratory activities) when you have been instrumental in ensuring that they already have a strong knowledge base and appropriate skills. Setting homework which requires a level of skill and understanding that has not been previously nurtured in school will result in frustration and a lot of hard work the following morning as anxious children (and, perhaps, parents) flood you with questions about how to complete the tasks successfully.

Keynote: To set homework which builds on existing foundations.

Pupil involvement in creating tasks is important

Some of the best challenges emerge from the children's own ideas and initiative. Their enthusiasm for pursuing learning will often be the spur for achieving effective outcomes. The highest levels of motivation occur when pupils are interested in what they are doing and believe that it is time well spent. However, even if you feel that you cannot rely on the children's ideas, you can sometimes offer them a choice from a limited menu of things that can usefully be done. The same homework does not have to apply to every child regardless of ability of aptitude; indeed, having a range of useful ongoing homework projects from which pupils can select over a period of time (days, weeks, half a term) often sit easily alongside more immediate ones. Parental involvement in homework is also more likely if the child shows genuine enthusiasm rather than grumpy subjection!

Keynote: To build on pupils' interests where possible.

Homework places additional demands upon teachers

Homework should be easily resourced and, wherever possible, self-assessed. Thirty pupils handing in thirty pieces of additional written work for marking and monitoring is a heavy burden to add to your existing workload. If you seek to involve parents in homework tasks, they will be keenly interested to know how highly their children achieved. This is sometimes due to the fact that some parents become so closely involved in the homework that they feel personally responsible for it (see TMS10). If homework is to succeed in helping children to learn more effectively, it has to take account of both logistical and parent-related factors (see also FPT, Chapter 3).

Keynote: To keep homework tasks manageable for pupils and teachers.

Homework can never compensate for poor classroom teaching.

Competence check

- [ ] My lessons provide a good foundation for extending learning
- [ ] I have considered pupils' ideas and suggestions when setting homework tasks
- [ ] The homework I have set is useful and appropriate

P4 Build on prior attainment to set clear targets for learning

(Section B, 4a, iv)

What you need to take account of to meet this standard ...

It takes time to establish what children already know

Although the requirement to discover what children already know sounds simple enough, it takes time and ingenuity. Class records offer some information but talking to the class teacher is the best way of finding out about individual children. A test score also gives some indication of ability but says little about qualities such as perseverance, cooperation and speed of work. The simplest method for finding out what children know and understand is through talking to them, asking questions and putting them in problem-solving situations where they have to draw on their existing knowledge. However, you need to be aware that some children do not know what they know! That is, although the knowledge is buried just beneath the surface, they do not possess the necessary communicative ability to transmit it to an adult (especially someone they do not know well). A number of shy children will conceal their understanding due to fear of getting things wrong or lacking the confidence to tackle more demanding tasks. If you are only in the school for a small number of weeks, it will take time before you get the full measure of a class and know the children well enough to set them appropriate work. This is part of *your* learning process.

Keynote: To take nothing for granted.

There are different forms of learning

Some lessons allow for specific learning outcomes; others are to do with attitude, collaborative skills and exposure to ideas in advance of gaining a full grasp of them. Learning may have to do with facts (such as multiplication tables) or uncertainties (such as where responsibility lies for wars). It may involve exposure to new ideas or consolidating older ones. Learning may require a specific skill (such as knowing how to shape a clay pot) or draw upon a range of skills (such as in science problem-solving situations). Pupils have to learn social skills (such as not interrupting when someone is speaking) and understand procedures (such as how to operate a computer). Some learning comes through being told directly; others through playing, experimenting or simply messing about. It is important for you to bear in mind that different forms of learning require different amounts of lesson time; thus, whereas telling pupils something may take moments, allowing them to discover things for themselves may require hours. On the other hand, telling them may result in only temporary grasp of the facts, while self-discovery generates more enthusiasm and secure knowledge if accompanied by appropriate adult intervention and explanation. Your lesson plans must take account of the nature of learning.

Keynote: To be clear about the prevailing form of learning.

Learning is never linear

Some children forget completely things they have learned; others require reminding; yet others never knew in the first place! It is difficult to distinguish children who did not grasp concepts during earlier lessons from those who had a tentative grasp but have lost some of their hold upon it. Learning is frequently more cyclical than linear. It needs to be revisited from different directions before it is firmly rooted. It is also well known for some children to 'jump' a section of learning and master more difficult material while struggling with (apparently) more elementary ideas. Although the expression 'prior attainment' has a safe ring to it, all teachers discover that learning is a difficult term to define and even harder to demonstrate. Your lesson planning has to make some assumptions about children's prior attainment or you would never plan anything. On the other hand, regular checking and monitoring of progress through question and answer and observation of the way that pupils deal with set work, will give a clearer picture than relying on a broad attainment level.

Keynote: To use various sources of evidence to assess the quality of learning.

Systematic teaching does not guarantee systematic learning

Building on prior attainment is not like setting a row of bricks upon one already laid; it is more like placing sticks on the glowing embers of a fire. You can prepare the most elaborate plans which respond to children's needs and take account of prior learning, organise and manage your lesson with great aplomb, yet find that some children have failed to grasp what you are teaching and require a variety of other approaches (sometimes less orthodox) to achieve the desired learning outcomes. Every lesson will consist of desirable learning intentions (those things that you hope that the children learn) and learning outcomes (those things that, in reality, they do learn). Sometimes the gap between intentions and outcomes is wider than is ideal. However, you can be sure that although some children will not learn exactly what you intended, they will learn things that you never intended, too.

Keynote: To be systematic in planning without being rigid.

You can take careful aim but discover a moving target

It is, of course, important to know what you are doing and why you are doing it, but it is foolish to set specific targets for learning which do not take account of changing circumstances and different contexts. If opportunities occur during a lesson to address important issues which were not in your original plan, it is normally worthwhile seizing them. Targets for learning cannot always be determined in advance; they often emerge as the lesson unfolds and the level of children's understanding becomes more apparent. A pre-lesson learning intention is not an immovable object; clues that you gain throughout the lesson about children's grasp of vocabulary, concepts, skills and the ability to apply them may significantly influence the time that you spend on a particular aspect of the lesson or the direction that you take. Lesson plans should not, therefore, be pursued irrespective of whether pupils understand what is happening. Although it takes a lot of courage and confidence to alter the direction of a lesson part way through, it is better than pursuing an inappropriate goal. For instance, you may discover that children do not possess the dextral skills that you anticipated and you will have to allow more time for them to practise; you might expect that they can complete a set task more quickly than they are able to and thereby have to postpone the lesson summary; you may find that a lot of children are making similar mistakes and have to stop the class while you repeat the explanation. If you are in the early stages of training and only have one chance to complete the lesson, you simply have to make the best of it. Gradually, you will improve your timing and expectations by paying careful attention to children's grasp of things as the lesson unfolds.

Keynote: To aim, fire and re-direct as appropriate.

Learning is a slippery process.

Competence check

- ☐ I am sufficiently aware of what pupils already know and what they have already experienced
- ☐ My teaching is well structured, yet flexible
- ☐ I have realistic targets for pupil achievements

P5 Identify and respond appropriately to pupils with learning difficulties

(Section B, 4a, v)

What you need to take account of to meet this standard ...

Learning difficulties are widespread

The majority of children have difficulty in learning certain skills or concepts. Even the most able children struggle from time to time, albeit at a higher conceptual level than less able pupils. Learning difficulties are not confined to core subjects. Some pupils struggle with rhythm in music lessons, orientation in map work, time sequences in history, designs in technology. Although the need to be able to read and write accurately and confidently is a priority, it is wrong to label children as having learning difficulties when they struggle in these areas without also acknowledging their expertise in other, less exposed aspects of learning. Similarly, it is rarely the case that academically able children are good at everything. Children may be perfectly capable of learning but have temporary difficulties due to factors such as bereavement, friendship issues or anxiety. Lesson planning cannot possibly take every factor into account but it pays to make a habit of looking out for pupils' uncertainties and misunderstandings across the spectrum of curriculum areas and keep brief notes about anything significant. Your lesson plans should take account of the need to remediate uncertainties through revising and reinforcing without losing sight of introducing fresh material. It is also important to distinguish between pupils who have a genuine lack of understanding and those who cannot be bothered to make the effort.

Keynote: To take account of pupils' lack of knowledge and misunderstanding in lesson planning and delivery.

There are short-term and long-term difficulties

Some learning difficulties are simply temporary blockages which require a slightly different emphasis in teaching approach or perseverance before they are removed; others are more chronic and seem to defy all attempts to help. Planning can take account of short-term problems through specific teaching for the group of children concerned; more deep-seated difficulties require longer-term strategies which may involve the school's special educational needs coordinator (SENCO; see SEN1). As a student on school placement, you can only play a small part in helping to rectify the longer-term problems by being aware of the individual education plans drawn up for individuals and taking account of their difficulties in your daily interaction with the class.

Keynote: To distinguish between temporary and chronic learning difficulties.

Pupils may have superficial or deep-seated learning difficulties

Learning difficulties range from broad ones such as 'generally weak at spelling' to particular ones such as regularly misspelling 'ie' and 'ei' words; the former is indicative of a deeply rooted problem requiring some specialist support, the latter can be dealt with by focused methods and deliberate targeting of problem words. Superficial learning difficulties can often be combated through intensive (and, if possible, enjoyable) teaching, together with additional homework and the support of parents. It is important that children who are struggling with superficial problems do not label themselves as failures in the subject (see TA5). For instance, children who misspell a few common words may start to call themselves 'useless' at spelling and gradually begin to convince themselves that it is true. Part of your job is to help children get things in perspective. You can help to enhance the positive classroom climate by adopting a 'you can do it' approach and helping pupils to gain in self-belief by offering them achievable short-term targets (Wassermann 1990).

Keynote: To diagnose the difficulty correctly.

Teachers cannot solve every learning difficulty by themselves

If the problems are severe, an appropriate response is to enlist the help of a more experienced member of staff; it is not necessary or desirable to try to deal with everything yourself. Some teachers have a 'learning difficulty' when it comes to enlisting help from colleagues! If you are a student, your class teacher will already be familiar with the scale of the problem and inform you accordingly. If a child's special needs have reached Level 2 (see SEN1) parents will also be involved in the process.

Keynote: To use all available expertise.

Learning difficulties can be deceptive

Some learning difficulties are due to the amount of time the pupil takes to gain understanding or mastery. For instance, some able children may be slow to grasp something but ultimately prove to have a more thorough grasp than those who achieved immediate success. It is unwise to jump to conclusions about a child's ability. Although some learning difficulties in basic skills stand out clearly, others take time to detect. Many children are also able to conceal their shortcomings by using a variety of strategies (see TA5). Learning difficulties may reside in the individual child, the nature of the task or the way you teach it. Some children may be experiencing difficulties outside school, and although there is some uncertainty about the impact that social conditions have upon children's ability to learn, every teacher knows that contented, happy children are more likely to achieve their potential.

Keynote: To take account of factors underlying learning difficulties.

> Regardless of their academic ability, all children are of equal worth.

Competence check

- ☐   I have a clear idea of individuals' specific learning difficulties
- ☐   I have taken account of these difficulties in my lesson planning
- ☐   I am drawing on suitable advice to help me cope with the demands made by individuals' learning needs

P6   Provide a clear structure for individual lessons

(Section B, 4b)

What you need to take account of to meet this standard ...

There is no such thing as an isolated lesson

A lesson should always link with what has gone before, while bearing in mind what lies ahead. Individual lessons are a convenient way of organising learning, but in reality learning takes place continuously at home and at school. If you are an inexperienced student, you may have to teach an isolated lesson as an introduction to lesson planning and management, but it would be folly to imagine that the classroom learning depends wholly on this kind of artificial separation.

Keynote: To view individual lessons within an overall framework.

A clear structure is not the same as a rigid one

The structure needs to be clear to you before it can be made clear to the pupils. You cannot hope to explain to pupils if you have not thought it through for yourself. Careful lesson preparation takes account of the likely order of events, the time that each phase of the lesson will take, the resources required, and the desired learning outcomes. Nevertheless, a lesson can take an unexpected twist for many reasons, including:

- the need to spend longer than anticipated on the revision section;
- children's responses to your questions or issues evoked as a result of their own questions;
- the length of time they take to complete the tasks;
- your awareness from monitoring the children's work that there is a widespread misunderstanding of something basic which requires immediate explanation;
- a general lack of motivation and enthusiasm. It takes a high level of professional judgement to decide when to persevere with the lesson formula that you so carefully prepared beforehand and when to deviate or even (in rare cases) abandon what you are doing.

Keynote: To be so well prepared that change can be accommodated.

The pupils are not privy to the teacher's thought processes

You may have spent a lot of time planning your lesson, but the pupils will be hearing about it for the first time. This necessitates a clear, firm and well-paced explanation rather than a hurried one. You should offer pupils the opportunity to ask questions about the tasks and your expectations for what they have to achieve (see TMS11). Pupils' questions range from basic ones which are for reassurance (so don't get cross if you have just told them that very thing!) to those which introduce creative ideas. Make your explanations pithy and convincing. Anticipate likely questions and have your answers ready.

Keynote: To let pupils know what is happening and what is expected of them.

Perfect preparation for every lesson is an ideal

Teaching, learning and assessment belong together. Your teaching should normally be accompanied by an indication of learning intentions and how you will monitor and assess the pupils' progress. However, no matter how well prepared you try to be, there will be occasions when you enter the classroom in a state of unpreparedness. At such times, the structure for your lesson should be as straightforward as possible. Sets of printed activities or text books can be invaluable as a short-term expedient. Experienced teachers sometimes rely on previous teaching occasions to bale them out of unprepared situations; students do not have that luxury.

Keynote: To strive for perfection while recognising reality.

A lesson structure provides a framework, not a blueprint.

Competence check

☐   My lesson preparation is orderly and comprehensive
☐   There is continuity between my present lesson and previous lessons
☐   The lesson purpose is clear to myself and the pupils

P7 Provide a clear structure for sequences of lessons

(Section B, 4b)

What you need to take account of to meet this standard ...

Every lesson is related to another lesson or lessons

Children learn from lessons in the same subject but also draw on other learning from areas which lie outside the immediate one. Such links are referred to as 'cross-curricular' and allow for the transfer of knowledge, skills and understanding between subjects (see P9). The more that you can refer to ideas and concepts established through other subjects, the more pupils will conceive of learning as a whole rather than fragmented parts. Phrases such as 'do you remember how ...?' and 'think back to the other day when ...' are useful spurs to establishing links.

Keynote: To exploit cross-curricular opportunities.

Lesson plans must be accommodated within the framework of curriculum planning

The longer the sequence of lessons, the less it is possible to write a lot of detail in advance. The school's medium-term plans offer a helpful framework, but the detail has to wait for the regular curriculum planning meetings between staff in the same subject area or age phase. Only then can your individual lesson plans be fully developed. The development of lesson plans must, therefore, take account of overall curriculum planning. In addition, no amount of pre-planning can allow for circumstances that may emerge over the time period of the lessons, so some modifications are inevitable.

Keynote: To see where lesson plans fit within the overall planning scheme.

Learning intentions should be considered before tasks and activities

A clear sequence of lessons must principally take account of the intended learning aims and objectives rather than activities to be done during those lessons. The activities should reinforce, develop and extend learning rather than act as a substitute. Lesson intentions can be gradually specified and linked with tasks and activities (see Figure 1). Bear in mind, however, that some learning emerges through activities such as play, problem solving and investigative work, not all of which can be predicted. Resourcing implications should be considered as the more free-flowing investigative activities may be curtailed due to lack of equipment or materials. Lesson plans can usefully be subdivided into three broad sections dealing with intentions, activities and resources.

Keynote: To consider intentions, then activities, then resources.

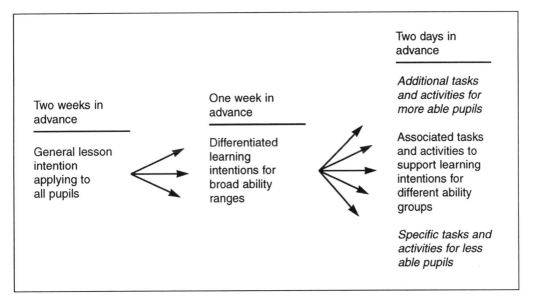

Figure 1   Increasing specificity in the planning process

Lesson sequences are subject to constraints

The danger of producing too many detailed lessons too far in advance is that they cannot take account of individual needs, the pace of learning and specific factors influencing the children's learning over time. Sequences of lessons (which are, after all, only strings of individual lessons) still need to take account of the differentiated learning needs of the whole class (McNamara and Moreton 1997). In practice, this requires a series of parallel learning intentions running through the series of lessons, something which is extremely difficult to maintain. A more practical approach to lesson sequencing is to have skeleton plans which can apply to the majority of children in the group or class and make more detailed plans nearer the time as the special needs and requirements become more apparent.

Keynote: To make advance plans which can be modified nearer the time.

Lesson sequencing is part of a rolling programme

Although many teachers plan for a half term, it is important to be constantly looking ahead and trying to predict possible trends and learning opportunities. For instance, an educational visit may be approaching which requires a special lesson focus; SATs tests, sports days or preparation for an assembly may involve disproportionately large chunks of time being devoted to that particular item. The availability of resources such as library packs and museum items may also influence the pattern of lesson arrangements. Sequences based on the National Curriculum programmes of study offer useful guidelines but cannot take account of individual school or classroom situations. Each subject area requires some element of advance planning and many lesson sequences can be based on the long-term curriculum programme; nevertheless, overlaps between subjects are both inevitable and desirable. Although it is important to draw up lesson plans in advance to provide a framework within which you can develop sufficient detail nearer the time, the need to look ahead requires constant vigilance.

Keynote: To take account of the unfolding patterns of school life.

> Sequences should be a guide, not a straightjacket.

Competence check

- ☐   I know exactly what I am doing this week
- ☐   I have a reasonable idea about the format of next week's lessons
- ☐   I have an outline framework for succeeding weeks' lessons

P8 Plan opportunities to contribute to pupils' personal, spiritual, moral, social and cultural development (PSMSC)

(Section B, 4d; Section 2k, xii)

What you need to take account of to meet this standard ...

Development is influenced by teacher–pupil relationships

Plans for PSMSC developments are not only located in a lesson plan; they are embedded within teacher–pupil relationships. Many studies have shown that pupils are more likely to learn effectively when working with a teacher whom they admire and respect. Pupils do not like teachers who are sarcastic, embittered or mean; neither do they think much of those who are poorly prepared and introduce uninspiring lessons in an unenthusiastic manner. Your life and conduct provides the single most significant influence for the pupils in their school experience.

If your pupils admire and respect you, they will be influenced by your opinions (Cooper and McIntyre 1995; Inman and Buck 1995). This is both a joy and a responsibility (see FPT, Chapter 1).

Keynote: To live out what we say.

Spontaneous opportunities may be significant

Opportunities for development exist within the planned and unplanned curriculum. Sometimes an older pupil's spontaneous, searching question can provide the basis for powerful discussions and provocative debate. Younger pupils can ask questions or make statements that are profoundly simplistic, thereby causing a lot of soul searching about fundamental truths. It is important to be as honest as possible, including acknowledging when you are uncertain, but be careful not to become trapped in conversations which are slightly unwholesome or unduly controversial. It is also quite easy to waste valuable lesson time talking about interesting but largely unimportant issues.

Keynote: To make good use of unplanned opportunities.

Personal development is individual

Personal development is largely about the kind of people we are: our actions, words, behaviour and maturity. There has been a considerable emphasis in recent years upon the rights of the individual. Your task is to acknowledge those rights but to inculcate a sense of personal responsibility, too. This can start in small ways in the classroom by promoting pride in its appearance, courtesy and caring, and allocating specific responsibilities to every pupil. As you value all children and their opinions (Suschitzky and Chapman 1998), you will also need to think carefully about helping them become more community orientated and good citizens. For example, children might be responsible for tidying one another's trays or be made a class monitor. A table-top inspection, involving every child in the group, with a recognised reward for the best (such as a small shield or flag) can encourage a sense of personal and corporate responsibility within the class.

Keynote: To promote rights and responsibilities.

Spiritual development touches the unseen

Spiritual development is concerned with dimensions of life which go beyond the immediate and visible, and provides a basis for pupils to clarify their views about life's meaning and its ultimate purpose. Some teachers claim that they have nothing to offer towards spiritual development as they 'do not have a faith' but this reticence is misplaced. We all believe something, even if it cannot be expressed using conventional spiritual terminology. The children in our care will be receiving a wide range of different messages from parents, friends, the media and religious groups about the deeper issues of existence and eternity. As their teacher, we have to help them make sense of what they hear at their own level of understanding. Every child can be led to appreciate the beauty of the natural world and be encouraged to see the worth of people they meet. All children feel the emotions of love and hate, and struggle with questions about why things happen, injustice and disappointment. You cannot impose your own perceptions and beliefs upon your pupils, but through structured sessions and informal opportunities you can help them to come to terms with difficult issues and feel more secure in a world where contradictory messages about the purpose of life abound.

Keynote: To help pupils to see that our lives have meaning and purpose.

Moral development deals principally with right and wrong

Moral development is concerned with forms of behaviour, attitudes to others and the rules of conduct which govern them. Moral norms have been challenged in recent years by those who claim that the only morality that counts is the one that is right for the individual concerned. As teacher, you first need to be clear about what you believe before you can help children to find their way through the moral maze. Although it is unwise to see yourself as an arbitrator in all things moral, you can uphold and promote fairness, respect, responsibility and compassion as central to the survival of every race and culture. If you are asked by children what you think about controversial issues, think hard before you answer; it is usually better to re-state your beliefs about basic principles of justice and harmony than to find yourself confronted by an angry parent wanting to know why you are leading the children astray with your outlandish views! The pupils in your class may not know precisely the difference between right and wrong, but they soon detect hypocrisy.

Keynote: To explore moral issues openly.

Social development is about our place in society

Social development is concerned with understanding the conventions of daily life and the structures which contribute towards good order and conduct. Pupils need to appreciate that community well-being depends upon reasonable conformity to social conventions. Some children come from backgrounds in which the conventions differ markedly from those in school. This presents particular difficulty for new entrants who often struggle with the contradictions between home and school. If you are a student working in someone else's classroom, you must familiarise yourself with the procedures, rituals and patterns of behaviour that the teacher has established, and try to maintain and strengthen them (Jones and Charlton 1996). If you are a newly qualified teacher, you need to establish your own rules as quickly as possible (see Table 2).

Keynote: To foster a cooperative climate.

Table 2 Establishing classroom conventions and procedures

Conventions and procedures need to be established in the following areas:
- conversation
- possessions
- movement around the room
- movement outside the room
- taking turns
- choosing
- team games
- volume of talk
- manners
- relating to adults
- care of equipment
- choosing partners
- the production of drafts and practice pieces
- the quality of final products
- dealing with finished work
- sharpening pencils
- going to the toilet

Cultural development is about the way that communities behave

Cultural development is concerned with how groups in society behave and relate to one another and to those outside the community. Pupils need to acknowledge and respect cultural diversity, while celebrating aspects of their own heritage. Children from minority communities are likely to have specific home influences which impinge directly upon their behaviour and attitudes. The school will have policies relating to religious adherence, such as what may be worn and when absence is tolerated. Children whose parents adopt unusual lifestyles and expect schools to accept whatever they decide may find themselves torn between wanting to support their family traditions yet not wishing to be marked out as 'different' by their peers. Sometimes tensions between customs and school rules can create problems for children and teachers in determining what is acceptable. Nevertheless, antisocial behaviour cannot be tolerated and instances of it should be reported to your supervisor or senior colleague.

Keynote: To take account of cultural diversity.

Development is a process not a product

Some teachers become discouraged if their pupils do not become the sorts of people they hoped for. In your work with children, it is important to remember that you are just one factor in the tapestry of influences which constitute their experience. Although your influence is important and may transform lives or at least make a substantial difference to children's attitudes and priorities, the final outcome rests largely with family influences and personal inclination. Your lesson planning and delivery should help to inform, provoke and stimulate an active interrogation of the issues, but never to indoctrinate.

Keynote: To do the best for each child.

Children judge our words by the way we act.

Competence check

- ☐   I am developing sound relationships with my pupils
- ☐   I am sufficiently clear about the different developmental patterns
- ☐   There is consistency between my curriculum programme and my own attitudes and behaviour

P9   Ensure coverage of the appropriate programmes of study

(Section B, 4e)

What you need to take account of to meet this standard ...

Some parts of the curriculum are optional and others essential

There is more flexibility in teaching history, geography, and design and technology than there is in teaching the core subjects of English, science, mathematics and information and communication technology (ICT). The core curriculum is formally assessed through SATs and therefore requires systematic teaching. The teaching of reading and numeracy should normally receive at least one hour's curriculum time per day. ICT is playing an increasingly important role in curriculum development and many schools have devoted considerable sums of money to ensuring that every child is computer literate. It is now a requirement that all student teachers possess a thorough grasp of how ICT is used in the classroom.

Keynote: To ensure that curriculum priorities are met.

Coverage does not necessarily equate with learning

The coverage of the curriculum does not guarantee that children have learned from it. Although teachers are required to follow the programmes of study, some areas need more thorough treatment; others can be dealt with relatively easily. For instance, the concept of time is a difficult one for many young children; older pupils often struggle with the procedures associated with long division. You will find that a greater proportion of teacher-led instruction and teaching 'from the front' results in faster coverage but does not guarantee effectiveness. Some learning cannot be hurried and needs a combination of direct teaching, practice, discussion and regular revision. In your records of pupils' progress it is easy to tick the 'have met' column after covering a curriculum area but much more challenging to know when to tick the 'met and understood' column to indicate pupils' grasp of subject knowledge.

Keynote: To discriminate between curriculum coverage and learning.

Cross-curricular opportunities must not be overlooked

Coverage is not only confined to working through a list of topics in single subject areas such as maths and English, but of seeing the potential for overlap and the place of cross-curricular elements, such as reading, problem solving, and the use of information technology. The more that children can see the links between areas of knowledge, the more they will perceive learning as a whole. Details of cross-curricular skills, themes and dimensions are listed in Table 3.

Keynote: To weave cross-curricular threads.

Coverage needs to be consistent across classes

Teams of teachers (teaching the same year group, for instance) have to move through the curriculum at approximately the same pace. Fortnightly team meetings are often used for such monitoring. Consistency is not, of course, identical to 'sameness'. Content coverage simply ensures that when all the children from the same age phase move up to their next classes, none will be disadvantaged. Your own enthusiasm and commitment to teaching should not, of course, be constrained by conformity.

Keynote: To keep in step with other teachers.

Coverage does not guarantee competence.

Table 3　Cross-curricular skills, themes and dimensions

Skills

These should be transferable and content free. Important ones include:

- communication
- numeracy
- study skills
- problem solving
- personal and social education
- information technology

Themes

There are five themes:

- economic and industrial understanding
- careers eduction and guidance
- health education
- education for citizenship
- environmental education

Dimensions

Based on the principle of equal opportunities and life in a multicultural society. Central principles involve the need for pupils:

- to be prepared for life in a multicultural world
- to fulfil their potential
- to have equal access to the curriculum

and for teachers:

- to avoid making unwarranted assumptions about children
- to safeguard equal opportunities

Competence check

- ☐　I am familiar with the relevant programmes of study
- ☐　I know what has to be taught
- ☐　I am focusing on pupil learning more than coverage of curriculum programmes

Chapter 2

Teaching Approach (TA1–6)

You must demonstrate competence in six areas of teaching:

TA1 Teaching of individuals, groups and the whole class.
TA2 Using teaching time.
TA3 Monitoring progress and intervening in pupils' work.
TA4 Establishing and maintaining a working environment.
TA5 Ensuring pupils' safety and confidence.
TA6 Ensuring pupils' acquisition of knowledge, skills and understanding.

TA1 Effectively teach whole classes, groups and individuals within the whole-class setting

(Section B, 4f); (see FPT, Chapter 7)

What you need to take account of to meet this standard ...

There is a difference between being efficient and being effective

Effective teaching should not be confused with efficient teaching. Effective teaching is largely concerned with product; efficient teaching with process. Effective teaching means that expectations are achieved or exceeded. Efficient teaching means that whereas the technical process of teaching is acceptably good, the learning intentions may or may not be achieved.

Keynote: To aim for effectiveness through efficiency.

What it means to teach the whole class effectively

You need to be clear about whether you are teaching the whole class as a single undifferentiated unit or whether you are responsible for a whole class which is divided up in particular ways (in collaborative groups, for instance) to achieve the desired outcomes. Effective whole-class teaching, especially when you are leading from the front, demands varied and engaging speech, interactive dialogue with the children through interesting questions, speculation and analogy, and the use of appropriate visual aids and board work. Interactive class teaching is a challenge for any teacher and requires a considerable degree of confidence.

Keynote: To involve the whole class in learning.

What it means to teach groups effectively

Group work takes many forms. Grouping can be for the purpose of organisation when all pupils are sitting in random groups, working independently. It can be based on academic ability, friendship, class control factors (such as separating troublesome children) or using a mixture for collaborative activities when diversity can be helpful. Groups may work on similar tasks with the expectation being that some groups will work more slowly or less successfully than others; or on different tasks which take account of the speed and ability of the groups. Whatever system of grouping you employ, it is important to be clear about why you have selected that option and how you will keep abreast of the demands that too much diversity places upon one adult in the classroom. Monitoring the progress of several groups, especially if they are involved in different types of task, can be very difficult. It is best to keep your organising for learning as straightforward as possible, especially in the early stages of working with the class.

Keynote: To group pupils in such a way that it benefits their learning.

What it means to teach individuals effectively

The final repository for all learning is in the mind and heart of the individual child. Whatever strategies you use to secure the learning, the main proof of your teaching effectiveness is the impact upon the individual. There are occasions when you can spend quality time with one child but these are rare and precious moments; for the most part, children learn alongside their peers and have to glean whatever they can as a member of a group or whole class. One useful way of checking that children understand or can do something is to ask them to explain or demonstrate to their peers.

Keynote: To consider the learning needs of individuals.

Teaching intentions need to be realistic

In order to meet all teaching intentions for the whole class, group and individuals, the number of objectives must be reduced and sharpened. Your teaching will need to be decisive and tightly bound. Too much curriculum task diversity places heavy demands upon your planning and organisation time beforehand, and your management and monitoring skills during the lesson. Student teachers and new teachers normally find that it is wise to restrict each lesson to a single curriculum area unless there is sufficient adult support available to allow for diversity.

Keynote: To organise for learning in a manageable way.

Good organisation is the key to success.

Competence check

☐ My lesson plan clarifies the different teaching approaches I intend to adopt throughout the session
☐ I am focusing on effectiveness as well as efficiency
☐ I have taken account of the way in which individuals learn

TA2 Meet teaching objectives through effective use of teaching time

(Section B, 4f)

What you need to take account of to meet this standard ...

There are many different time constraints

Making the best use of the available teaching time requires that you consider:

- the time that is formally available according to the timetable;
- other demands upon children's time such as movement between locations, longer than expected assemblies, play rehearsals, outings, illness, and so forth;
- the time spent on lessons, which may not equate with learning, as the most memorable learning experiences are sometimes short and dramatic. Other learning provides 'fertiliser' to the roots of the main lesson purpose and helps to promote learning, despite its 'invisible' nature;
- the teaching time used for specific teaching of literacy and numeracy.

Although time constraints can be problematic, they can also help you to sharpen your organisation and set yourself targets for completion and achievement.

Keynote: To be sensitive to time factors.

There is a danger of confusing 'busyness' with learning

Using too much direct teaching without the necessary fallow times necessary for reflection, thinking, re-consideration and the raising of questions is counter-productive. You should develop opportunities for pupils to give 'yes but' responses and, where appropriate, probe complex ideas rather than passively accept them. There is, however, a need to be careful about random exploratory activities which use up a lot of time but achieve little, and convoluted problem-solving activities which substitute for well-constructed experiments. Although prospective parents visiting a school may be impressed by a quiet class, heads down, concentrating on the work in hand, a closer inspection of the learning taking place might show that there is more froth than substance.

Keynote: To use learning time effectively.

Time can be wasted through inadequate preparation and poor classroom organisation

Tasks such as sorting out groups and setting out resources should be done beforehand wherever possible to save wasting valuable lesson time doing it. If pupils are left hanging around while you fiddle and scramble around, the lesson gets off to a poor start which may be difficult to retrieve. There is no substitute for thorough preparation as a means of ensuring that the lesson goes well. It is essential to think through every stage of the lesson and anticipate possible problems and opportunities, such as children who have to attend other lessons part-way through, interruptions for watching TV programmes and the act of distributing resources. Time, tide and restless children wait for no one (Arnold 1990).

Keynote: To prepare well and organise in advance.

Time can be wasted through the use of inappropriate teaching methods

If a direct-teaching approach can achieve the same results as exploratory methods, it makes sense to use it. On the other hand, if a concept or skill needs to be practised and absorbed, there is little point in merely telling pupils when they need to experience it for themselves. Some teachers spend time unnecessarily in asking pupils low-level questions or asking them to 'read my mind', going from one child to another in an attempt to find one person who knows the correct answer. Although questioning technique is a powerful means of promoting thinking and stimulating ideas, it should be used alongside imaginative transmission teaching (see TMS6). Similarly, a lot of teachers have a habit of spending too long talking without involving their pupils; consequently, the time and energy expended results in limited learning as bored children gaze ahead vacantly.

Keynote: To use appropriate teaching methods.

Teaching time can be affected by non-teaching time

Your duties do not end at the classroom door. There are meetings to attend, playground and bus duties to perform, parents to speak to, telephone calls to make.

There are colleagues to contact, tutors to inform, resources to gather and children to advise. All these factors influence your ability to prepare for sessions, get to classes in good time and mentally adjust to the demands of the classroom. Teaching time cannot be isolated from the teacher's wider professional responsibilities; nevertheless, you must try and ensure that teaching time is protected and used as effectively as possible.

Keynote: To take account of non-teaching pressures.

> We all have the same number of hours available in the day.

Competence check

☐   I have taken account of time factors in my lesson planning
☐   I have organised my teaching in such a way as to avoid time wastage
☐   I am aware of other ways in which time might evaporate

TA3 Monitor and intervene when teaching to ensure sound learning and discipline

(Section B, 4g)

What you need to take account of to meet this standard ...

Knowing how to monitor and when to intervene requires considerable skill and professional judgement

Monitoring and intervention are concerned with both behaviour and learning, though the two are often related. Inexperienced teachers find it difficult to keep track of everything that goes on in the classroom. Older hands seem to spot some things before they actually happen! Monitoring is not separate from the act of teaching; it has to take place at the same time. You may discover that you are so involved in your interactions around the classroom that you fail to spot those children who are making little effort or those struggling with the work. Subsequent intervention can take many forms, including a decision to leave a situation alone. Good teachers are aware of what is happening and let the pupils know they know.

Keynote: To stay alert to what is happening throughout the classroom.

Teaching approach influences the monitoring of learning

Transmission teaching (teacher talking; pupils listening) allows for easier monitoring of behaviour but gives the teacher little information about how much the pupils are learning. Monitoring is more straightforward when the pupils are involved in a set task which leaves the teacher free to circulate, offer advice, ask questions and actively engage with the learning to find out how pupils are progressing. Reactive forms of teaching (when the pupils respond as directed) require that teachers use questions to probe the pupils' understanding or ask for responses as a means of testing their conceptual grasp of issues. Some difficulties may occur through children calling out or getting over-excited. Interactive teaching (initiated by the teacher but where pupils are encouraged to contribute at will) are hardest to control but often give valuable information about pupils' understanding as they attempt to express themselves freely.

Keynote: To utilise different forms of monitoring.

Observed behaviour cannot be relied upon as an accurate indicator of pupils' understanding

The quiet child who looks puzzled and does not offer any suggestions, even when invited, may be ignorant of the facts or may need time to think or may be too inse-cure to say anything (Collins 1996). Such situations are commonplace. Similarly, the child who gives an incorrect answer to a question may not know the answer or may be working to a different agenda. Younger children, in particular, will some-times affirm loudly that they understand things when, in reality, they are giving a conditioned response which they believe will satisfy their teacher. While you will wish to closely observe children's actions, it is often only by talking to them and allowing them to talk, that you discover their true understanding (see TMS8).

Keynote: To observe carefully and listen attentively.

Monitoring and assessment are closely related

Only when pupils are given time to address issues and challenges through practi-cal work, written output, speaking and listening, diagrammatic representations or skills-based processes can you make an accurate assessment of their learning. Even then, with the passage of time, revision and recapping of events and principles will often be needed before learning can be judged to have been satisfactory. Monitoring pupils' progress is a continuous process.

Keynote: To monitor as a means of enhancing formative assessment.

Intervention depends on various factors

If the purpose is to allow pupils time to engage with difficult issues that defy easy resolution, or the establishment of cooperative groups to collaborate and debate the issues, intervention is best delayed until children have had opportunity to engage with the challenges presented by the lesson. Broad issues about when and where to intervene have to be considered alongside the practicalities of how much support to offer and, in a busy classroom, how much time to spend with individuals, groups and the whole class. It is sometimes desirable to leave children to struggle on with their work rather than intervene too quickly and not give sufficient opportunity for considered thought and grappling with uncertainty. On the other hand, if pupils are left to struggle for too long, they may become restless or disruptive. In the worst scenario, failure to intervene may result in a loss of motivation or loss of class control. You cannot rely on appropriate and successful intervention to ensure an orderly environment if other factors, such as the interest level and relevance of the subject matter, has been neglected (see FPT, Chapter 9).

Keynote: To time interventions carefully.

Appropriate intervention is more than responding to signals for help

Some pupils are afraid to ask for help and require sensitive handling; others view teacher support as failure and resist help even when it is offered; yet others rely too heavily on support and benefit from some time alone before being rescued. Some pupils develop a dependency upon the teacher which can become obsessive, thereby failing to realise their true potential. Whether this is due to fear of failure or has some deeper meaning is not fully understood. One way or another, intervention should not act as a substitute for pupils thinking for themselves. Before you offer your support, think about whether those children asking for assistance could, with prompts and encouragement, gain more by battling through their uncertainties than passively receiving answers from you.

Keynote: To avoid over-dependency.

Intervention does not have to come from the teacher

Pupils cannot learn for others but they can help others learn for themselves. In collaborative settings, the combined knowledge and wisdom of the group can be a positive means of reinforcing learning and helping individuals through their particular struggles. Peer support can suffer from the same constraints as adult intervention, and there are additional problems concerned with the distraction that may be caused to the more able pupil when constantly providing advice to the less able. Parents are sometimes anxious if they believe that their children are being used as a pseudo-teacher. Nevertheless, you will save yourself a lot of time and give pupils opportunity to share their knowledge and skills if you foster a climate of mutual support and cooperation (see TMS1 and TMS11).

Keynote: To encourage a collaborative classroom environment.

> Monitoring and intervention should enhance learning.

Competence check

- ☐ I am carrying out effective monitoring of work and behaviour patterns
- ☐ I am giving careful thought to my intervention strategies
- ☐ I am taking note of the reliance that each child places upon my intervention

TA4 Establish and maintain a purposeful and secure working atmosphere and a good standard of discipline through well-focused teaching and positive and productive relationships

(Section B, 4h, i)

What you need to take account of to meet this standard ...

A purposeful and secure environment takes time to achieve

If you are a student teacher on placement in someone else's classroom, it will take perseverance and courage to establish and maintain a purposeful and secure environment (see FPT, Chapter 2). Students enter classrooms in which the class teacher has, it is hoped, already established the right sort of climate. The student teacher's task is, in large measure, to maintain it rather than establish it. However, if you are meeting groups of children for the first time, you still need to let it be known to pupils that you intend to promote the same rules and expectations that they have been used to with their regular teacher. And don't be lulled into a false sense of security: however delightful the class appears to be initially, the testing time will come. A no-nonsense approach is essential if you are not to spend most of your time on school placement trying to retrieve a situation that you allowed to run out of control by being too passive early on. It is important not to become discouraged if you struggle initially. Establishing a purposeful and secure working atmosphere and good discipline will also depend upon pupils' previous experiences of teachers and their motivation to learn, so some things are beyond your immediate control.

Keynote: To insist on standards of behaviour.

Pupils take time to adjust to different expectations

As a student teacher, you need to recognise that pupils have become used to their own class teachers' expectations and priorities, so it is wise to adopt the same approach initially. Over time, as you become more familiar with the classroom situation, you will be better able to introduce small changes in the working environment. You may find that in trying to establish your expectations, some pupils become confused or anxious, even protesting that your way is 'not the way it is done here'. Patient, consistent and firm explanation about your expectations and the way you want things done are essential. However, if you are unsure whether you may be unintentionally transgressing school procedures, it pays not to be too insistent until you have checked it out.

Keynote: To insist without being arrogant.

Relationships are built not imposed

Good relationships evolve through shared experiences, clear expectations and rules which are fairly and consistently applied. Above all, pupils do not want to be humiliated, nagged or blamed. Your positive approach, interesting personality and love of learning will help you in your quest for good teacher–pupil relationships. Nonetheless, pupils feel more secure when they are convinced that you know what you are doing and are capable of handling the lesson. They need to be convinced that they have more to gain from cooperation than from lethargy or mischief-making. Children will take note of how you relate to individuals (especially the troublesome ones) and your reactions at critical moments. Clear learning objectives, proper resourcing and thinking ahead to predict possible problems, all contribute to a positive working environment.

Keynote: To build productive and positive relationships.

The best type of discipline is self-discipline

All pupils need clear guidance about what constitutes appropriate behaviour, but ultimately they have to decide for themselves that they want to learn more than they want to misbehave. However, some pupils appear incapable of exercising self-discipline without regular insistence from an adult. So don't be afraid to be precise and firm about your expectations. The ideal is to move from a position where pupils do what they are told because you insist, to one where they do so because they choose to. All children need to be reminded from time to time that they are responsible for their own actions and that you expect them to set high standards for themselves (see FPT, Chapter 9).

Keynote: To encourage pupils to be responsible for their own actions.

Well-focused teaching can also be imaginative

As a simple test of what constitutes well-focused teaching, consider whether the average parent, sitting in on your lesson, would understand what you were trying to achieve. In doing so, it is important not to equate being specific with unimaginative teaching methods. On the contrary, the most effective lessons are those in which you use a variety of teaching strategies to achieve the intended aim. If you can capture children's imaginations and appetite for learning by introducing relevant, interesting lessons, you will rarely meet severe discipline problems (see Figure 2).

Keynote: To be a creative teacher.

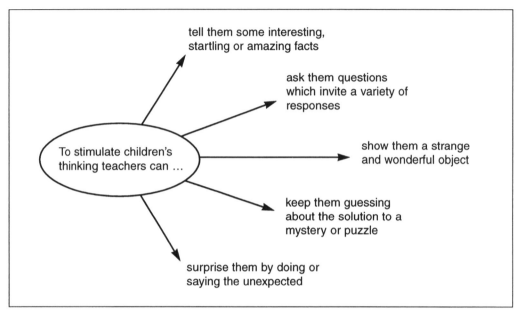

Figure 2   Stimulating pupils' thinking

An effective working environment comes through determination and perseverance.

Competence check

☐   Pupils understand what I expect from them
☐   Pupils feel that I am in control of the situation
☐   The quality of my teaching minimises the likelihood of disruption

TA5 Establish a safe environment which supports learning and in which pupils feel secure and confident

(Section B, 4j)

What you need to take account of to meet this standard ...

The meaning of a safe environment

A safe environment is one in which pupils feel that the teacher is in control, that they will be able to do their best without having to contend with undue interference from others, and where their efforts will be acknowledged and recognised (see P2 and TMS7). Pupils feel safe when they are protected from bullies, given equal opportunity to use resources and allowed to make genuine mistakes without fear of the consequences. A safe environment is one in which adult–child relationships are courteous, respectful and caring (Noddings 1992). Pupils will not feel safe if they experience humiliation, sarcasm, hectoring or persistent nagging. It is your job to try to provide a learning environment in which lessons are appropriate to the needs of the children, where you explain your expectations clearly, and where you deal with disputes, concerns and upsets in a calm and determined manner. In short, you are both the instigator and the guardian of a safe environment.

Keynote: To allow all children to fulfil their potential.

The limitations of your own influence

Although you may feel that you could engender a much healthier atmosphere by adopting a different approach to teaching and learning from the present teacher's, you will not be able to affect the situation markedly in the short time you are in school, and it is more sensible to adopt a strategy of compliance rather than trying to exercise an assertive form of professional autonomy. In short, try to fit in rather than turn the situation upside-down. Accept the class situation as you find it and recognise that you can have a modest but significant impact upon the working environment in small but important ways, rather than being able to transform the situation. When you are the class teacher you will want students to build on existing structures rather than trying to upset the classroom equilibrium; so be sensitive in your attempts to 'establish' a secure environment.

Keynote: To comply enthusiastically.

Learning and a secure environment should be linked

A secure environment does not necessarily lead to effective learning. Pupils can feel secure without necessarily making a lot of progress. Teaching approaches are sometimes divided into those where teachers are concerned with the affective dimension (that is, developing a close, caring relationship with pupils) and those concerned with the managerial dimension of the role (that is, focusing on attaining measurable outcomes). However, while it is true that different teachers emphasise one or the other, the two dimensions should be seen as closely entwined (like a tapestry) rather than at opposite extremities. The most effective learning takes place when pupils are motivated to work for their own benefit and out of respect for and loyalty to the teacher.

Keynote: To manage pupils' learning skilfully and caringly.

Confidence is a delicate flower

Some children are naturally confident. They seem to ooze self-belief and will have a try at anything. They are first to shoot their hand in the air when you ask for a volunteer and seem to relish challenges. Nothing daunts them. Other children are hesitant and prefer the seclusion of anonymity. They have to be encouraged, cajoled and enticed to take a risk. A fear of failure or humiliation handicaps their learning and suppresses their potential (see P5). Most children lie somewhere between the two extremes and may be confident in one situation and hesitant in another. Equally significant is the way in which the same child may be less confident with another teacher; similarly a child who lacks confidence with one teacher may be much more willing with a different teacher who is perceived as gentler or more patient. It is not difficult for teachers to wreck children's confidence through adopting a harsh and unrelenting attitude. It is also true that your understanding and positive manner can help to repair or raise a child's damaged self-esteem. Merry (1998) suggests that children's responses to the likelihood of failing may take many forms, including regression to more infantile and helpless behaviour or venting their frustration on a weaker child. Merry also suggests that children use a variety of strategies to offset the pain of failure (see Table 4). You have to learn to discriminate between those pupils who are too idle to attempt the work and those who are sincerely troubled by concerns over failure. Careful explanations about tasks and appropriately differentiated work will help to offset the worst avoidance problems. If they persist, you may need to spend additional time with the particular children but without making them too heavily dependent upon you.

Keynote: To respect children's sensitivities.

Children think a lot more than they speak

Some children are slow to express their feelings to a teacher. Even when children are feeling uncertain, confused or bewildered, they will rarely confide in a teacher unless things become critical, by which time it may be too late to rectify the problem. Students sometimes find out things that are not disclosed to the regular teacher because they are perceived by pupils as being less threatening. This is not

Table 4 Pupils strategies to avoid failing (based on Merry, 1998)

- Pupils produce the first answer that comes into their heads
- Pupils only do the easy bits (such as a picture) and neglect the more demanding parts of the work
- Pupils wander around the room while the teacher is occupied with others
- Pupils find reasons to leave the room, especially going to the toilet
- Pupils blame the task, using expressions such as 'This is boring'
- Pupils deliberately avoid listening so as to be genuinely confused
- Pupils do nothing until they are assisted by the teacher
- Pupils work very slowly and make minimal 'safe' progress
- Pupils cheat
- Pupils lose their work, either by destroying it or misplacing it

invariably true; sometimes students may themselves be under-confident and fail to establish a satisfactory relationship with the children. Nevertheless, the principle that positive attitudes towards children lead to trust and openness is something that every adult working in school should know.

Keynote: To take account of pupils' deeper feelings.

> Children are more likely to trust you when they feel that you are in control.

Competence check

☐ I have developed a positive working climate in my classroom
☐ I have established a sensible balance between the managerial and affective dimensions
☐ I am evolving teaching strategies which ensure that all children have opportunity to make optimum progress

TA6 Ensure that pupils acquire and consolidate knowledge, skills and understanding in the subject

(Section B, 4m)

What you need to take account of to meet this standard ...

Ensuring is a tough requirement

As a teacher, you can make every effort to help pupils acquire knowledge, skills and understanding, but you cannot ensure that what is apparently mastered at one time will be carried forward into new learning. Sometimes, pupils understand something sufficiently well for them to deal with the work in hand, but they do not have an adequate grasp of it to use their learning in new situations. That is, they have failed to create the necessary links between distinct, but related, circumstances. Ensuring that pupils acquire and consolidate knowledge, skills and understanding has to be interpreted in terms of the context and the language competence of the child. Your teaching approach needs to take account of pupils' past experience of learning, the knowledge, understanding and skills that they have gained, their interest in the subject matter. It is worth remembering that two pupils who superficially appear to have grasped something will still vary in their ability to apply and extend what they have learned.

Keynote: To ensure that pupils are given the best opportunity to enhance their knowledge, understanding and skills.

Knowledge and understanding depend upon perceptions of reality

A nine-year-old might find out that bombs fell on the town during the Second World War, but it is only by speaking to the elderly lady living down the road who survived the onslaught that the knowledge is transformed from a passive piece of information to a dynamic reality in the child's mind. Even then, the child is unable to hear the whistle of shrapnel, the cries of fear and the smell of cordite. Pupils will, depending upon their own experience, imagination and ability to internalise facts, construct an image of bombs falling and causing destruction in the town. The elderly resident will have a more direct form of knowledge due to her lived experience, but may, over time, have created a distorted picture of reality in her mind. Indeed, it is fair to say that if both the child and resident could, in some miraculous way, be transported to the event itself, they would have slightly differing tales to tell of the same situation. Although there are some building bricks of knowledge which necessarily provide the foundation for extended learning, children have to be taught to examine the facts in the light of fresh understanding and experience. The knowledge that you pass on to your pupils will sometimes be absolute and sometimes open to interpretation. Children's understanding relies on the sense that they can make of the evidence with which they are presented and the associated factors that impinge upon the circumstance. As you seek to enhance pupils' knowledge and understanding, it is important to see things as children of that age see them. Ask for their opinions, listen to what they say in reply and take note (see also TMS10).

Keynote: To take the children's perspective into account when organising for learning.

Consolidation can be achieved by various means

Consolidation of indisputable facts may best be achieved by repetition; for instance, generations of children have learned their multiplication facts in this way.

Consolidation may involve fuller understanding of facts; for instance, the effect of placing a letter 'e' after the final consonant of a word containing 'a' softens the centre vowel (mat becomes mate; rat becomes rate, etc.) but the rule does not operate with every vowel (pot does not transform to pote; get does not become gete, and so on). By looking at the fuller picture, discussing the variations and enjoying the nonsense words, the original facts become more meaningful and memorable. Consolidation may involve using existing knowledge, skills and understanding in problem-solving or investigative situations; for instance, orientation and mapping skills can be utilised for an environmental project based around the school grounds. All forms of consolidation are enhanced by talking to others about the subject area involved. Many people testify to the fact that they never know that they understand something until they hear themselves explaining it to someone else! (See Figure 3.)

Keynote: To consolidate without confusing.

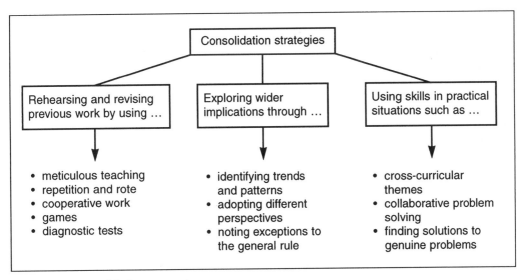

Figure 3 Consolidation strategies

There are degrees of understanding in everything.

Competence check

☐ I know what knowledge and understanding I want the pupils to acquire
☐ I have taken sufficient account of pupils' age, experience and present understanding
☐ I have incorporated a valid and reliable means of assessing pupils' progress into my planning

Chapter 3

Teaching Methods and Strategies (TMS1–12)

Teaching methods and strategies involves the largest number of statements. There are 12 areas in which you must demonstrate your competence:

TMS1 Using teaching methods which result in optimum pupil performance.
TMS2 Matching the approach to the subject and pupils.
TMS3 Structuring the lesson.
TMS4 Presenting key ideas appropriately and imaginatively.
TMS5 Instructing, demonstrating and explaining.
TMS6 Effective questioning.
TMS7 Using pupils' errors and misconceptions.
TMS8 Listening and responding to pupils.
TMS9 Acquiring the necessary basic skills and study skills to utilise learning resources.
TMS10 Offering opportunities for pupils to consolidate their knowledge.
TMS11 Setting high expectations for all pupils.
TMS12 Developing pupils' wider understanding.

TMS1 Use teaching methods which sustain the momentum of pupils' work and keep all pupils engaged through stimulating intellectual curiosity, communicating enthusiasm for the subject being taught, fostering their enthusiasm and maintaining their motivation

(Section B, 4k, i)

What you need to take account of to meet this standard ...

Teaching methods form part of a total teaching approach

A 'method' suggests a single, specific and definable way of doing things. However, the best teaching methods are sufficiently structured to provide a solid framework for the passage of the lesson and sufficiently flexible to allow for unexpected opportunities. Some inexperienced teachers find that a particular method works in a certain situation and assume that it can be used in every situation, regardless of context or conditions. It is not uncommon to hear comments such as 'I use stand-and-deliver methods' or 'I rely on group work' or 'I get the children to discover things for themselves'. All of these methods (and many others) are useful but it is unwise to think of any one of them as the answer to a teacher's prayer. The best teachers employ a variety of methods appropriate to the occasion. Table 5 offers some guidelines over making your decisions.

Keynote: To employ a range of teaching methods.

Table 5   Determining the appropriate teaching method

- To give information: use direct transmission
- To examine issues: use explanation followed by discussion
- To teach techniques: use demonstration followed by skills training
- To develop study skills: use explanation followed by activities
- To consolidate previous learning: use activities and tasks
- To extend thinking: use group investigation
- To develop oracy: use group problem solving

A method depends on the person using it

Although teaching methods are based to an extent on following familiar procedures and strategies, their effectiveness relies on the quality of your preparation, delivery and competence (see FPT, Chapter 6). Some teachers are very effective in a 'stand-and-deliver' mode and can keep the pupils' attention through variety of tone, use of visual aids, stories, poems and lively questioning. Others find that their skills lie more in developing and supporting group activities; yet others will provide interesting worksheets which stimulate and probe pupils' understanding, and so forth. The very best teachers do all of these things. Wherever your talents lie, it is worth exploiting them fully and demonstrating your abilities openly. In areas of teaching where you feel less confident (such as taking the 'up-front' role) it is worth persevering and getting some advice about how you might improve (Hayes 1998).

Keynote: To utilise teaching strengths fully and address weaknesses resolutely.

Interesting lessons require a special effort

Intellectual curiosity is stimulated when pupils' interest has already been engaged and they believe that it is worth making the effort to find out more. You can enhance this interest by projecting a lively curiosity of your own as you introduce lessons and engage with the pupils' learning throughout the lesson. Deadpan expressions and lifeless monotones are certain to create an inert learning climate. Relevant and interesting lessons have to be presented in attractive ways if children are to be convinced by them. Every child is curious, so exploit their curiosity at every opportunity. Place items in boxes; hide things from sight until the last moment; present the mundane in unusual ways; heighten expectation; celebrate discoveries. Don't forget that things which are commonplace to grown-ups can be a source of delight for young minds. Although it is not advisable to adopt a 'song-and-dance' mentality towards teaching, it is preferable to incline in that direction than being grim and unsmiling.

Keynote: To capture pupils' interest by teaching with flair and imagination.

Pupils' and teachers' motivation vary

In an ideal world, motivation would remain consistently high. In reality, levels are unpredictable and fluctuate from day to day, lesson to lesson, and even during a single session. Motivation is controlled by a complex mix of lesson content, pupils' previous experiences of the subject, your own enthusiasm and the embedded expectations about teaching and learning that exist in the class and throughout the school (see also TMS11). Some days, teaching is like stirring treacle; on others, it is like hang-gliding. Predicting that some lessons will be a struggle, or explaining why some are successful, is difficult, but it is worth being alert to some of the most powerful influences that may affect lesson planning and delivery (see Table 6).

Keynote: To motivate oneself first of all.

Table 6 Motivation factors

High motivation is likely when:
* teachers and pupils feel happy and relaxed
* the subject matter is interesting and relevant
* teachers have experienced recent success in their teaching
* the classroom climate is safe and secure
* pupils believe that they will be treated fairly
* expectations are clear and achievable
* success is visible and celebrated

Problem solving can be a powerful medium for harnessing the collective wisdom of the group

The lesson purpose is not always about cleanly defined learning intentions; outcomes are frequently far messier than could have been envisaged, particularly when collaborative tasks and dealing with complex and unpredictable dilemmas form the heart of the session. Problem solving is not a substitute for teaching; it is an opportunity for pupils to use the knowledge and understanding which they already possess and exploit them to find answers to questions. There are two broad forms of problem solving: one in which the answer is genuinely unknown (the 'what will happen if' type) and one where the answer is known by the teacher but not by the pupils (the 'find out what the answer is' type). In the first case, a variety of answers may be possible, in which case the problem solving is more correctly called 'investigating'; in the second case, it is likely that there will only be a single or small number of possible solutions (see Table 7). It is important that you ensure that before children are given collaborative tasks of any kind, you have spent time explaining the ground rules and attitudes required for successful completion (see FPT, Chapter 7).

Keynote: To involve pupils in the collaborative effort.

Table 7 Problem solving and investigations

- Problem solving: where there is a problem to be solved which may have only one or a strictly limited number of solutions
- Investigations: where there are a variety of possible solutions

---

Effective teaching involves relationships, instinct, personality, creativity and perseverance.

Competence check

- ☐ I am willing and able to use a range of teaching methods
- ☐ I have taken account of pupil motivation
- ☐ I am able to enthuse the pupils by my teaching

TMS2 Match the teaching approaches used to the subject matter and the pupils being taught

(Section B, 4k, ii)

What you need to take account of to meet this standard ...

It is sometimes easier to match the teaching approach to the form of knowledge than to the curriculum subject

A lot depends on what you expect the children to learn. For instance, if you want them to acquire specific knowledge for a limited period of time (i.e. knowledge that only has to be remembered for a limited time, such as a specific safety procedure during an educational visit) you will want to explain what is required as quickly and firmly as possible, and monitor the situation until the need to remember has passed. If the knowledge is required over a longer period of time, your approach depends on the type of knowledge it is. For instance, things to be memorised demand a different teaching approach from things that can be found out through reference. Whereas the knowledge to be memorised will benefit from repetition, discussion, committing the facts to paper, and so on, information from references requires an understanding of where to look for it, what forms of information to access (books, the Internet etc.) and how to translate the information into useful knowledge. It is relatively easy to find out the date and outcome of a famous battle; it is more demanding for pupils to understand its impact on people's lives and its place in the sequence of events of that time. Although some subjects tend to invite a particular teaching emphasis, the end product of what you want the children to learn and the best way for them to achieve it should dominate your thinking more than whether you happen to be teaching a particular curriculum subject (Littledyke and Huxford 1998).

Keynote: To use the teaching approach which facilitates learning.

Some learners benefit from practical tasks

Younger children generally benefit from having plenty of opportunity to touch, feel, examine, experiment and discover for themselves. This does not mean that they are incapable of storing information and understanding, but that structured and unstructured play is a valuable way of reinforcing learning and allowing them to extend their thinking. However, involvement in practical activities will not, of itself, ensure enhanced learning. It needs to be part of a total learning programme. There are broadly two ways to approach using practical tasks to assist learning. The first is to introduce topics to the pupils and help them to develop a basic understanding through explanation, examples and demonstration, then set practical tasks as a means of confirming the truth, exploring alternatives or consolidating learning. For instance, to demonstrate that the perimeter of a polygon is the same regardless of whether the measures are taken clockwise or anti-clockwise, then set practical tasks to confirm the validity of the claim. The second approach is to set a problem-solving task at the start of the lesson, giving a strict time limit, then to draw on pupils' findings to establish the principles or key facts. For instance, children may be given the task of finding the speed at which different objects (screwed-up paper, cork, feather, paperclip, conker) fall to the ground (on to a thick newspaper to avoid too much noise!). Subsequently, you can garner all the differing findings and opinions and discuss the laws of gravity and, perhaps, the effect of air pressure on some objects. Children normally enjoy practical tasks but you have to try and ensure that the time is well spent. (See Figure 4.)

Keynote: To set purposeful practical tasks.

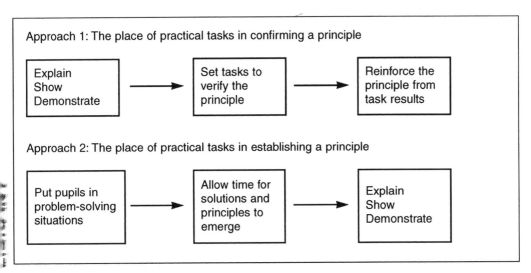

Figure 4   The place of practical tasks in learning

Organising for learning requires a knowledge of the individual pupil

You have to make a decision about whether pupils will learn more effectively through individual or collaborative activities, bearing in mind that the children who like to work alone are sometimes the ones who need to experience working in groups. Persuading children to work in groups who prefer to work alone requires a lot of tact and firm encouragement. Children who fear to work alone should not be allowed to rely too heavily on other pupils or yourself. More enterprising lessons should involve a mixture of individual, pair and group activity, even if it has to cover a number of sessions. For instance, session one might involve considerable teacher input followed by individual work, session two might involve working in pairs, session three might involve collaborative problem-solving tasks. Whatever form of organisation you use, always take account of its manageability and the need to make things clear to pupils concerning the times they are expected to work singly and when they are allowed or encouraged to work with a partner. Forms of organising may look slick on paper but flounder because the needs of particular pupils have not been fully considered. For instance, some children get confused about the distinction between collaborating and cheating.

Keynote: To take account of individual needs and inclinations.

Different teaching environments require different approaches

Teaching in a classroom-based situation requires different skills from those required in a large-space situation (see FPT, Chapter 7). Organisation has to be extremely thorough and well planned for large-space activities as there are no activity options available in the way there are in the classroom. In the classroom, there are normally paper-and-pencil activities, small games, finishing-off tasks and book resources to use. In the hall it is a matter of being involved or not involved (by sitting and watching) with all the potential for misbehaviour that the situation brings.

Keynote: To take account of room size.

> The most important question to ask is how pupils learn best.

Competence check

- ☐ I am taking account of the subject area when I plan my teaching
- ☐ I incorporate the appropriate mix of direct teaching and practical activity
- ☐ I have made allowances for the particular learning needs of individuals

TMS3 Structure information well, including outlining content and aims, signalling transitions and summarising key points as the lesson progresses

(Section B, 4k, iii)

What you need to take account of to meet this standard ...

Information comes in different forms

Some information is for identification purposes (such as the name of a piece of equipment); some is for guidance (such as ways of using the equipment); some is to establish parameters (such as limitations on the equipment's use); some is speculative (such as possible creative uses for the equipment). It is worth using these subheadings in planning and presenting the facts.

Keynote: To distinguish between different types of information.

Information should not be confused with knowledge and understanding

Information has to be interpreted and evaluated before it can be absorbed into a pupil's knowledge system and used actively in learning. For instance, children can learn a song off by heart in a foreign language yet not understand a word! Some children love to accumulate information but have little idea about its use and relevance. If you provide information to pupils, try to explain its significance by using a number of practical examples or demonstrations to consolidate learning. Ensure that they have time to talk about the information and handle it in a variety of ways (through worked examples, practical tasks, etc.) until they see where it fits in with their existing knowledge.

Keynote: To aim for fuller understanding.

Structure alone is insufficient

Content is an important factor in lesson planning but relies upon an active teaching approach to engage the pupils' hearts and minds. It is wise to spend a small amount of time telling pupils about the broad structure of the lesson, together with what you hope they will achieve, what they have to do, how long they have to do it, and where it links with other aspects of learning. Basic details can be written on the board or a sheet of paper in advance of the lesson (an example is given in Table 8). Interactive teaching, in which you allow for pupils' questions and reactions, invite opinions, and stimulate thinking, needs to be balanced with periodic summaries of 'so far' and 'therefore'. Your explanations should be well paced and clear, allowing adequate time for pupils to absorb what you are saying and, where relevant, ask for clarification. Regardless of the extent to which lessons are structured, teaching should be active and dynamic, allowing opportunity for pupil involvement and creativity. If the structure is sound, creativity can flourish; if it is unsound, creativity becomes chaos!

Keynote: To develop a purposeful lesson structure.

Table 8 Example of a lesson structure

Topic
Designing and describing products (design and technology)

Number of people
Individually, then in pairs

Task
1 On your own, construct a simple structure from the materials provided that can stand upright without support (10 mins)
2 Write down instructions to make it, using only five steps (10 mins)
3 Give your partner the instructions to follow (10 mins)
4 Watch as your partner makes the structure (5 mins)
5 Discuss how to improve the instructions (5 mins)
6 Write up the new instructions plus a diagram of your model on the clean paper provided

Extension
Incorporate the newly discovered ideas into the 'Inventions' project

---

Transitions may be planned

Your lesson plan may involve an introduction in which you remind pupils of what has gone before; a short and lively question-and-answer session to stimulate interest; an explanation about the lesson content; a demonstration of correct equipment use; opportunity for questions, comments and points of clarification; collaborative tasks as a means of exploring the relevant concepts and mastering the key skill. The skill with which you move from one lesson element to another will influence the overall lesson success. It is relatively easy to change from (say) time spent on direct-transmission teaching to a question-and-answer session; it is far more difficult to move from direct teaching to the associated practical tasks. It is important to remain fully in control during this transition and give firm, clear and decisive instructions to children about where they should go and what they should do. Avoid the 'scrummage' approach in which you give instructions and then release the children like a bullet from a shotgun as they pepper around the classroom to begin their tasks. Allow only a few children to move at one time, ensuring (of course) that resources are available and adequate for the numbers involved.

Keynote: To keep a firm grip during transitions.

Transitions may be unplanned

However closely defined your lesson preparation may be, there are occasions when your instinct tells you that it is time to move on to another phase. Such moments are signalled when, for instance, the children are getting restless or enthusing about new ideas or suggesting creative possibilities. You have to decide whether to 'go with the flow' and respond to their behaviour, or to maintain the lesson pattern as you originally conceived it. Although pupils should never be allowed to dictate the pattern of a lesson, wise teachers take careful account of their actions and reactions, and adjust accordingly.

Keynote: To take account of the learning climate.

Summaries should be succinct

A summary should be just that! Resist the temptation to launch into new ideas. The end phase of a lesson is always quite demanding, requiring a variety of class-room management skills – summarising the lesson purpose, praising good work and effort, dispensing information about where to put finished and unfinished items, maintaining control, observing the time and ensuring that the room is left tidy – so resist the opportunity to present a tide of new ideas in the final few minutes. End on a positive note but do not allow children to leave the room until you are satisfied they have completed what is required. Stay alert until everything is orderly, then dismiss the children as appropriate (see FPT, Chapter 9).

Keynote: To pay as much attention to the end phase of a lesson as any other.

Thorough preparation builds confidence which releases creativity.

Competence check

☐ I am clear about whether I am dealing with knowledge or information
☐ I have structured my lessons in such a way as to allow for a smooth transition
    from one stage to the next
☐ There is room in my lesson for creativity and innovation

TMS4 Clearly present content around a set of key ideas, using appropriate subject-specific vocabulary and well-chosen illustrations and examples

(Section B, 4k, iv)

What you need to take account of to meet this standard ...

Key ideas should link closely with lesson intentions

Content may take the form of factual information, the introduction of ideas, problem-solving situations, experiments, reinforcement activities or a combination of elements. If your lesson is principally concerned with introducing new vocabulary or examining the structure of certain words, the key ideas will be different in kind from one in which the purpose is to master specific practical skills or follow set procedures. A useful way of establishing the key ideas is to try to describe them in a single sentence to someone who knows nothing about the subject.

Keynote: To link content with lesson purpose.

Accurate and appropriate use of vocabulary is essential if pupils' understanding is to be extended

Pupil puzzlement over terminology is an obstruction to learning. Do not assume that pupils know the meaning of terms, especially subject-specific ones. Spend a little time towards the start of the session introducing or clarifying important words, and throughout the lesson providing necessary explanations. Understanding terminology requires more than being familiar with regular terms; pupils need to be able to handle concepts by using appropriate vocabulary. For instance, in maths pupils need to know the names of common 2-D and 3-D shapes before they can discuss their properties. Words such as 'pitch', 'duration', and 'tempo' are significant when it comes to discussing musical excerpts.

Keynote: To integrate vocabulary with concept development.

Illustrations and examples need to be chosen with care

Younger children tend to accept things literally and find it difficult to interpret metaphors. The challenge is to use appropriate vocabulary that conveys the concept, idea or information for children in a way which is appropriate to their different ages. Examples should be as precise as possible rather than using analogies or inexact comparisons. Primary-age children accept most things literally; they have neither the maturity nor intellectual sophistication to be able to generalise an example to the particular. This is especially true when attempting to explain deeper truths about moral and spiritual values. For instance, reference to death as someone 'falling asleep' or 'going to heaven' may conjure confusing images for younger children who might fear going to bed at night lest they never wake up or imagining heaven to be full of corpses! Similarly, the expression 'as cunning as a fox' will have a different meaning to town and country children. Even traditional tales about 'wicked step-mothers' take on fresh meaning for children from split homes who now live with a new family.

Keynote: To take account of children's maturity when using examples.

Terminology should be used consistently and accurately

For instance, the terms 'take away', 'subtract' and 'minus' have a common meaning when used in respect of finding the difference in size between two numbers; but have subtly different meanings when used in specific circumstances. Thus, 'take away' indicates removal of a part from the whole, whereas 'subtract' relies on a comparison between two numbers and 'minus' is used in connection with negative numbers. Similarly, the word 'tone' has a different (though associated) meaning when used in art and music. Some terms are exclusive to the subject; where else except in English, for example, are we likely to refer to adjectives and pronouns? However, if terminology is to be used effectively, we must ensure that words are used consistently and understood by the children.

Keynote: To establish a common vocabulary.

Words are tricky things.

Competence check

- ☐ I have thought carefully about the key ideas for the lesson
- ☐ I am using appropriate vocabulary for the age and ability of pupils
- ☐ I have chosen my illustrations and examples with care

TMS5 Offer clear instruction and demonstration, and accurate, well-paced explanation

(Section B, 4k, v)

What you need to take account of to meet this standard ...

Effective teaching needs thorough preparation

The most effective direct teaching results from thorough preparation and rehearsal. It is a mistake to imagine that teachers are good 'on their feet' due solely to natural ability. Most effective transmission teaching requires a strong grasp of the relevant facts and their implications, and time spent beforehand considering the best way to deliver the lesson in a meaningful way which allows the children to absorb what is being said. It is one area of teaching that can be usefully rehearsed beforehand, preferably recorded on an audio cassette. Listen out for the moments of hesitation which indicate uncertainty and the variety in your tone of voice. Make a deliberate effort to 'write in' pauses (count to five in your head) and anticipate the kinds of questions which children may ask after listening to you. Although a lesson structure may vary from your planned intention, thoroughness of preparation is never wasted (see Figure 5).

Keynote: To prepare thoroughly for direct teaching.

It is essential to clarify the type of direct method you are adopting

Broadly, there are three approaches. The first is when you are transmitting infor-mation, using interesting and visual stimuli where appropriate. Second is a reactive approach in which you pose the questions and problematics for pupils' to consider and make response towards. Third is an interactive approach in which pupils are able to interrupt, ask their own questions, offer insights and comment without your sanctioning it (see also TMS1).

Keynote: To clarify the form of direct method used.

Effective didactic teaching benefits from a dynamic delivery

Instruction and demonstration demand a direct-teaching approach in which the teacher initiates and controls the pace and content of the lesson. You should make it clear to pupils whether you want to speak uninterrupted, whether you want them to respond in some way (and if so, how), or whether they are allowed to make comments, offer suggestions, raise questions, and so forth. If you are speaking uninterrupted, then the use of an assertive voice, variety of tone and appropriate visual aids are important elements in maintaining pupils' interest and attention. Didactic teaching allows you to project your personality and develop a good

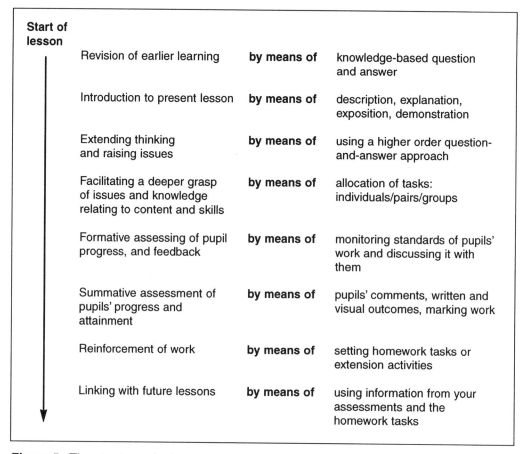

Figure 5   The structure of a lesson

rapport. It also invites unwanted comments and restlessness if delivered poorly or is unduly extended.

Keynote: To speak with verve and enthusiasm.

Pupils take time to absorb what teachers say

Although you may have spent many hours preparing your lesson, the pupils will be hearing things for the first time. It is therefore essential to explain things carefully and in a spirited manner but without rushing. Small pauses to allow pupils the opportunity to think about what you have said or clarify points will enhance learning. Some children who appear to be uncooperative are trying to make sense for themselves of your confusing instructions. If one line of reasoning or explanation does not appear to be working, it is worth trying a different approach rather than endlessly persevering with the same one. It is easy to get carried away by the sound of your own voice and forget for whom the explanation is intended!

Keynote: To consider the listeners.

Demonstrations require particularly careful preparation

Demonstrations are of two broad types: those in which you are showing something to pupils because it is the best way for them to learn; those in which you are showing basic skills for pupils to use later in their own practical activities. Before commencing a demonstration, it is essential to have resources near at hand, to stand where all pupils can see and hear, and to have key words and ideas written beforehand on the board or cards (to reduce the amount of time spent with your back to the class writing things down). Before you show pupils how to do something, it is important to be sure that they have already mastered elementary ideas, skills and vocabulary associated with the topic.

Keynote: To know what is being demonstrated and the practicalities of carrying it out.

Making things clear to pupils is a top priority.

Competence check

☐ I have thought through exactly what I am going to say and how I am going to say it
☐ I am speaking at an appropriate pace with adequate pauses
☐ I am injecting some vitality into my teaching

TMS6 Provide effective questioning which matches the pace and direction of the lesson and ensures that pupils take part

(Section B, 4k, vi)

What you need to take account of to meet this standard ...

Questions form an important part of teaching

Your lesson preparation should place questions you intend to ask under three basic forms: those for which there is only one answer; those for which there are a limited number of correct answers; those for which there are a variety of possible answers depending on individual opinions. Good questions stimulate thought, create interest, encourage pupils to think, explore ideas and consider alternatives. As questioning involves an interactive form of teaching, make certain that you have good class control and some basic rules of courtesy and procedure. If you ask a question to which there is no definite answer or where you are uncertain, it is better to say so at the start rather than trying to give the impression that you know everything; however, make certain that you find out the answer as soon as possible or guide the children to do so on your behalf. You will benefit from showing as much enthusiasm for finding out as you expect from your pupils.

Keynote: To use questions constructively.

Questions can seem threatening to pupils

Some children stick their hand in the air at every opportunity. Others become nervous about answering questions publicly and it may be a long time before they feel confident enough. It is, of course, essential to treat all answers seriously, even if they are incorrect, as an abrupt response to children's tentative responses may damage their confidence for a long time. A useful way of gaining pupils' trust, and allowing timid children to gain some reflected glory from their confident peers, is to wait until someone provides the correct answer, then ask the rest of the class who else knew the answer, commending them accordingly as the hands are raised. Alternatively, if there is a single answer to the question, give two possible endings (one correct, one incorrect) and ask those who think that the first answer is correct to wink at their partner; then those who think that the second is correct to wink with both eyes. After you reveal the right answer, ask those who guessed correctly to raise their hands. If the question invites a variety of answers, write all of them on the board as they are suggested by the children, number them, and take a vote about which answer is most convincing. Allow the children to vote for (say) three of the answers and draw up the first, second and third choices overall. Although you cannot maintain this complex approach indefinitely, it will help children to appreciate that questions are meant to assist them in knowing and understanding rather than catch them out. By treating all answers seriously (other than on those occasions when children are being deliberately silly, when it is best to ignore them) you give pupils a signal that you value their willingness to try. A cold, dismissive or abrasive response will indicate to more timid pupils that it is better to keep quiet than to incur your wrath.

Keynote: To take account of pupils' concerns in framing questions.

Teachers tend to ask questions for assessment purposes

It is rare for teachers to ask questions because they genuinely do not know the answers and believe that the pupils can provide them! The majority of questions are used as an assessment tool whereby the teacher wants to see how well pupils respond to questions based on the work in hand. Assessment questions to which there is a single answer should be used as a means of checking that pupils understand and reminding others about the facts. You should take special note of pupils' answers which indicate that further work is necessary in the area covered by the questions.

Keynote: To use assessment questions sparingly.

Questions can be used at a variety of levels

It is best to use straightforward questions initially, followed by more involved and challenging ones which can be introduced as pupils are reminded of fundamental points and grasp basic concepts. For instance, you may ask a question about the name of a mountain range (Snowdonia, say) and about the name of a range of hills (Brecon Hills, say) which probe the distinguishing features of a 'mountain' and 'hill'. Depending on the age of the children, further questions may invite answers about characteristics of hills and mountain ranges, their composition and use (recreation, water-power supplies, wildlife, and so on). With careful prompting, children quickly provide stories and instances from their holiday experiences, programmes they have seen and books that they have read. At the end of this interactive time, it is important to return to the fundamental questions which underpin your lesson objectives. For example, it is interesting to know that Elizabeth saw a baby lamb on her weekend walk, but does little to extend the class's understanding of weathering and erosion if this was the key element of the lesson!

Keynote: To layer questions conceptually.

Pupils should develop a questioning attitude

Teachers have a responsibility to create a questioning environment by valuing pupils' questions. Pupils will ask questions when they are interested to know the answers. They will become interested when you engage their hearts and minds and provide lessons which stimulate and enrich their intellects. You will know that you are succeeding in creating such an atmosphere when children become desperate to find out and are willing to persevere and ask questions publicly to do so.

Keynote: To stimulate a desire in pupils to discover more.

Some questions are unanswerable

Learning to live with uncertainty is something that primary-age pupils find very difficult. Issues tend to be clearly defined in their minds and it may take a long time for them to appreciate that dilemmas and paradoxes are as much a part of life as clear-cut solutions. In ethical and moral areas, in particular, it is worth spending a little time in explaining alternatives to children or allowing them to offer opinions before attempting to provide satisfactory answers. Children have to learn to accept that some questions do not have a straightforward answer and others do not appear to have any!

Keynote: To embrace uncertainty.

Questions should not be used as a precursor to a telling-off

If pupils associate questions with subsequent scoldings, either because they did not know the answer or because they were admitting to an inappropriate action, their attitude to questioning may be damaged. Such instances include: asking a question and telling off the child for not knowing the answer; asking a question with a threatening tone and, when the child admits responsibility, rewarding honesty with nagging; asking a question and sighing or making a sarcastic comment at the child's expense. In cases of indiscipline, it is tempting to use such a harsh tone when enquiring about the circumstances that only the most courageous children would dare own up. Consequently, children are tempted to lie and spend the next few minutes defending their innocence against a chorus of accusations from fellow pupils. By asking the question in a moderate, non-threatening but serious tone, it is more likely to receive an honest reply. Even if the child admits to something naughty, approve their honesty without detracting from the seriousness of the behaviour by prefacing what you say with words to the effect: 'Thank you for telling me the truth, but I think that you know that what you did was wrong ...'.

Keynote: To use questions positively.

> Thinking people ask thoughtful questions.

Competence check

☐   I am clear about my reasons for using questions
☐   I am using a variety of open and closed questions
☐   I am encouraging children to adopt a questioning approach

TMS7 Pay careful attention to pupils' errors and misconceptions, and help to remedy them

(Section B, 4k, vii)

What you need to take account of to meet this standard ...

Mistakes are a natural part of learning

The saying that 'the person who has never made a mistake has never made anything' is a useful maxim for classroom learning. If pupils are made to feel that there is no room for error in their work, they are likely to become defensive or refuse to attempt things for fear of getting them wrong (see TA5). It is important to make the distinction between mistakes which occur as a result of negligence and those which come from misunderstanding or ignorance. Children who earnestly strive to do their best should be praised and encouraged; those who are apathetic or slothful are, of course, less entitled to sympathy.

Keynote: To put mistakes into perspective.

Pupils like to get things right

It is not always easy to persuade children that mistakes are inevitable and can be used positively. Younger children, in particular, love to see a page of ticks, smiley faces and 'well done' comments. You may need to work hard to convince pupils that although it is preferable to get things correct, it is better to try to get things wrong than not to try at all. A lot depends upon the type of work being undertaken. For instance, if children are attempting to find the answers to a number of computation problems, their ability to find the correct answer is axiomatic to the lesson. In such situations children are pleased to do well and deserve congratulation; however, a raw score may not tell the whole story, for some children may do less well because they have been prepared to attempt more innovative methods to arrive at the answer which will, in the long term, provide the basis for a deeper conceptual understanding of the process. It is easy to emphasise the number of correct answers to such an extent that those children searching for alternative solutions may revert to the tried and tested ways to avoid being stigmatised as failures. In your enthusiasm to see pupils gain increasingly higher marks, do not overlook the courageous minority.

Keynote: To put correct answers into perspective.

It takes time to get to the root of mistakes

It is tempting to correct mistakes without finding out why the error was made. Asking the child to explain his or her thinking is a powerful means of understanding pupils' thought processes and adjusting your teaching on future occasions. If a child reveals a flawed understanding, a brief clarification will often suffice. There are occasions, however, when a longer explanation will need to form part of a future lesson. The problem with large classes and a busy schedule is that teachers often do not have the time or opportunity to ask questions which probe pupils' understanding; consequently, teaching becomes a mechanical process of setting tasks, marking the results and assessing the children's progress solely on that basis. If you develop the habit of asking pupils about why they have proceeded in particular ways, you will gain unexpected insights into their thinking.

Keynote: To get to the root of pupils' errors.

Determine the error's significance

Making a decision about what is significant requires a great deal of professional judgement. A lot depends on the lesson's intentions. For example, a spelling mistake is significant if the lesson is largely about correct English but relatively insignificant during a brainstorming session when ideas are being thrown down on paper. Similarly, misreading a portion of text may be vitally important when mastering vital health and safety information but relatively unimportant when reading a humorous tale. You may decide to overlook mistakes if pointing them out would disrupt the proceedings unnecessarily, as you can always return to the mistake at a later stage if necessary. On the other hand, to allow an error to remain unchallenged may, in some cases, allow wrong ideas to become embedded in pupils' minds. It can be helpful to preface an intervention with words to the effect: 'Well done to get so much correct. May I point out one thing that you have got confused about ...' or similar.

Keynote: To differentiate between serious and trivial errors.

Misconceptions are more serious than forgetting

Everyone needs to be reminded about things from time to time and everyone makes errors on occasions. It is relatively easy to remind pupils of the correct answer or procedure, or to give them advice about how to find things out for themselves. It is more difficult to remedy a misconception because the wrong idea may have taken root. It is worth listening quietly while the child tells you what she or he thinks as a means of discovering where the misconception lies. Once this is established, the process of rectifying the problem can begin.

Keynote: To distinguish between pupils' conceptual and memory problems.

Remedies take differing amounts of time

A casual error (e.g. incorrect punctuation or multiplication) can be corrected quite easily. Indeed, many children will often self-correct if you ask them to look again at their work. More substantial errors may reveal a wholly wrong or confused understanding about the subject. In this case, it will take time to revise previous concepts, re-teach forgotten skills or educate into ways of thinking. The five-year-old who holds a pencil incorrectly can be shown the proper way until, with gentle reminders and appropriate demonstrations, the problem soon passes. By contrast, the ten-year-old who cannot tell the time is going to need a lot of help. Children who do not grasp fundamental skills and concepts will rarely catch up quickly, despite your endeavours on their behalf, though it is possible that your carefully worded explanation and response to a pupil's elementary questions can lead to a sudden surge in understanding. Most of teaching involves continuous effort and application, including a willingness to spend time on a one-to-one basis with the pupil, set and mark specific homework and involve parents where appropriate.

Keynote: To take account of time factors in remedying mistakes and misunderstandings.

If one child has misunderstood, it is certain that others will have, too

When a pupil's error comes to light, it is rare for other children to admit that they share the uncertainty or misconception. More often, the other children who have made similar errors will attempt hurriedly to conceal their mistakes by rubbing out what they have written or changing their response. This defensive reaction results in superficial and contrived improvement which fails to tackle the underlying problems. The pupil's willingness to admit their mistakes is one indicator of the strength of the teacher–pupil relationship. Take note of any error which you notice in several pieces of work and either deal with it by stopping the whole class and talking about the matter there and then, or incorporating it into the next suitable teaching session.

Keynote: To be alert to pervasive problems.

Significant errors should be recorded in writing

It is important to make a record of significant errors, for three main reasons: so that you can adjust future lesson plans accordingly; to give yourself opportunity to reflect upon their significance when you evaluate your lessons; to consider what they tell you about ways in which you might improve your teaching. They also assist you when it comes to formal assessment of pupils' work for reporting to parents. It is unwise to assume that you will necessarily remember things. Find a way of making a rapid record in advance of writing it down more carefully after school, such as carrying a small notebook, having a piece of paper stuck on the back of the stock cupboard door or using a dictaphone.

Keynote: To use the assessment of errors as a basis for recording and reporting to parents.

Mistakes are inevitable. It's the final product that counts.

Competence check

- ☐ I have a positive attitude towards pupils' mistakes
- ☐ I have taken time to analyse the underlying cause of the mistakes
- ☐ I have a firm idea about the number of pupils who struggle with similar difficulties

TMS8 Listen carefully to pupils, analyse their responses and respond constructively to take pupils' learning forward

(Section B, 4k, viii)

What you need to take account of to meet this standard ...

A speaking and listening classroom has to be developed

Some teachers discourage children from speaking other than when given permission. Other teachers believe that free and natural speech is essential for effective learning. You have to decide what you are prepared to allow. If you want pupils to have opportunity to speak, you will need to structure your lesson in such a way that it facilitates their contributions within an orderly framework. Finding a balance between encouraging pupils' verbal expression and maintaining an orderly climate is not easy; however, insistence upon basic rules such as not calling out, taking turns and waiting until others have finished speaking provide a helpful structure within which speaking and listening can be enhanced. Student teachers must be careful to take note of what the class teacher presently allows and making gradual changes to the interactive pattern after consultation.

Keynote: To encourage constructive talk.

There are different ways to take pupils' learning forward

Pupils can learn facts, understand concepts or gain skills. They can also learn about tolerance, uncertainty, dilemmas and relationships. Learning may take the form of 'learning how to learn' or where to access information or when to speak and when to remain silent. Learning, therefore, encompasses a range of social, practical and cerebral skills from the quality and form of teachers' responses. The nature of your response acts as a marker for pupils' perceptions about what needs to be known and understood, and what kind of interactions are acceptable in the classroom.

Keynote: To see learning as a journey.

Teachers sometimes talk too much

If you talk too much, pupils will listen to your words but not really hear what you are saying. They may nod their heads and sit bright-eyed looking in your direction, but information overload will deaden rather than kindle their enthusiasm for learning. Some inexperienced teachers find it difficult to sustain a period of transmission teaching; others say too much. Whatever is said, however, you must use appropriate vocabulary and pitch your words at a conceptual level suitable to the age and ability of the children.

Keynote: To speak concisely.

Teachers sometimes fail to listen to what pupils say

Classrooms are busy places and it is tempting to half-listen to what pupils say (Brown and Wragg 1993) rather than understand what they are trying to tell you. Many teachers find that in order to hurry things along they interrupt children and put words in their mouths rather than allowing them to express things in their own way. Children who are struggling to frame their words will need special patience. Stern (1995) suggests that it is damaging to teacher–pupil relationships if teachers go through the motions of listening without really doing so. Real listening involves teachers trying to understand pupils when what they say makes little sense, accepting the pupil's viewpoint even when they disagree and giving their full attention to what the pupil is saying. Pupils appreciate teachers who give them support but trust them to deal ultimately with the issues, give space for mistakes to be made and offer them enough time to think things through thoroughly and make their own decisions.

Keynote: To be an active listener.

Constructive responses lead to improved understanding and motivation

Constructive responses involve learning to hear what pupils are saying 'beyond the words themselves' and offering encouragement for them to persevere with what they are trying to express through positive body language (such as nods and smiles) and comments (such as 'yes' and 'I understand what you're trying to say'). Children need to know that they are being taken seriously, so the more that you can use their ideas as a basis for developing discussion or shaping the work, the more they will feel that it is worth taking the risk of offering an opinion. Even unusual verbal contributions can provide a stimulus for further debate and clarification of the position. It is sometimes worth checking that you have understood what a child has said by responding with, 'Are you saying that ...' and re-phrasing what they have said. It is, of course, possible to respond unconstructively, with a resulting deterioration in motivation. Pupils do not appreciate being hectored and lectured on the altar of teachers' frustrations.

Keynote: To value pupils' contributions.

Talking and listening are equally significant.

Competence check

- [ ] I am encouraging constructive classroom talk
- [ ] I am really listening to what the children are saying
- [ ] I am setting a good example with my own use of language and talk

TMS9 Exploit opportunities to improve pupils' basic skills in literacy, numeracy and IT, and the individual and collaborative study skills needed for effective learning, including information retrieval and good use of text books

(Section B, 4k, ix and xi)

What you need to take account of to meet this standard ...

Basic skills are age and ability related

Basic skills evolve and develop as pupils become more sophisticated in their understanding and experienced in their knowledge application. However, most foundation skills need to be revised and reinforced regularly to remind pupils of their significance and ensure that they are firmly embedded in their thinking. Although some younger children may be well advanced academically, they are normally less mature than older children of similar ability. In grouping for learning, especially in classes with more than one year group, there is a need to consider both academic and maturity elements.

Keynote: To take account of competence and maturity.

Some study skills are essential

Study skills rely heavily upon pupils' ability to read, discover facts, classify information, and record appropriately. The ability to skim and scan is particularly important and requires regular, structured lessons to ensure that pupils have an increasingly thorough grasp of it. The Literacy Hour often is based around sections of a relevant text which form the heart of a whole-class lesson lasting between 45 minutes and one hour. The acronym used to describe the structure of the lesson is DARTS, standing for Directed Activities Relating to Texts (see Figure 6). Similarly, unless pupils are capable of manipulating number bonds, they will struggle with many areas of mathematics, and the Numeracy Hour is intended to support this key objective.

Keynote: To build strong foundations.

Individual study skills involve confidence and independence

The availability of information is only one element of gaining knowledge. Once access to the information has been secured, pupils have to be trained and directed about ways of recording and using their newfound knowledge. Although it may not be prudent or realistic to write everything down or print everything out, the search for knowledge is most effective when it influences decisions and ideas. Some children take time to gain confidence in their own judgement and require

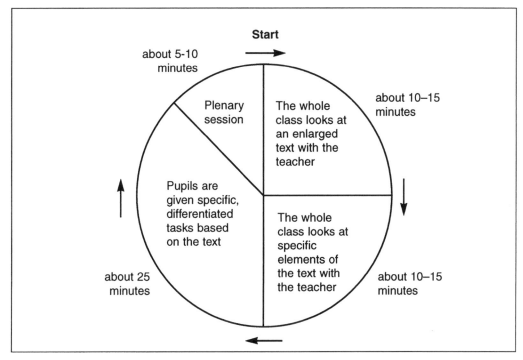

Figure 6 Directed activities relating to texts (DARTS)

careful guidance from an adult or another child before they risk committing anything to paper. Others assume that they must use every scrap of information which is slightly relevant to the topic. You have the difficult task of ensuring that every child has sufficient confidence and discrimination to know where to look for information and process what is found. Confidence will grow as you systematically teach study skills; independence comes as you give pupils opportunity to develop their skills through access to information sources (see Table 9).

Keynote: To cultivate self-responsibility for learning.

Table 9 Developing independence in learning

Children need to know and understand the following:
- where to look for information and advice
- how much adult support is available
- how long to persevere before seeking help
- what to do with information once it has been found
- how much to record
- how much to share subsequently with others

Information technology is a significant contributor to learning

The growth of information and communication technology in recent years has led to the establishment of computer-generated systems in all schools. Children often have machines at home and become adept at handling technology, especially programs involving a fun element. Teachers need to be vigilant to ensure that the enjoyment of using the technology is not at the expense of its principal function; namely, to act as a knowledge source. Pupils will require as much guidance over selection as those using more traditional written sources of information. Although computers have brought benefits in terms of the way they allow access to information, their appeal to children who struggle with conventional forms of recording ideas and their graphic capability, it is important to be alert to a number of potential disadvantages: the over-use of the computers by a small number of children at the expense of others; the possibility of time-wasting with programs of a relatively low conceptual level; the loss of traditional writing and drawing skills. Although many primary schools are becoming more technologically sophisticated, there are important classroom management issues to consider, including equal opportunity, monitoring the amount of time pupils spend using equipment, safety factors (including the danger of eye strain) and the location of resources. If equipment is located in special bays or rooms outside the main classroom area, lesson organisation needs to take special account of supervision factors. Information technology, like every other contributor to learning, must be used effectively. You should no more let children loose with computers without adequate training and supervision than you should with books, science equipment or hockey sticks!

Keynote: To make effective use of IT equipment.

There will be wide variance in pupils' experience of ICT

It is important to be aware that some pupils have a greater understanding and experience of information and communication technology (ICT) than their teachers. Children may spend many hours on their home-computer system, especially playing games, sometimes aided and abetted by a parent or an older sibling. By contrast, school technology can seem quite dull and constraining. Other pupils will not have access to computers at home, so their experiences at school become even more significant. Computer-literate children may try to dominate the use of machines in school; on the other hand, it is useful to be able to draw on their expertise whenever possible. Use of information technology not only has to be differentiated in terms of the programs used but must also take into account the experience, confidence and expertise of individual pupils.

Keynote: To assess pupils' ability and aptitude with IT.

Resources must be available and accessible

Careful classroom organisation and procedures for taking care of equipment and associated teaching aids are essential if learning is to be enhanced. Care needs to be taken over the siting of equipment, safety factors and maintenance. Faulty equipment is a source of frustration and can consume your time when you need to concentrate on other aspects of a lesson. Even basic resources need to be properly managed: a tin full of blunt pencil crayons is little use to anyone! If a large amount of equipment is being used (such as different types of balances for work in maths) you have to make the decision about whether to place the balances on tables in advance of the children coming in to the classroom or distributing them after you have introduced the lesson. In the majority of cases, it is better to have items out of reach until they are needed. Attention to detail pays dividends in facilitating a smooth-running lesson.

Keynote: To think carefully about resource implications.

Text books have a variety of uses

A text book may or may not be useful in your teaching and depends principally upon your lesson purpose. Some books are poorly written, inappropriate or confusing; the majority offer some help but are rarely perfectly aligned to what you are trying to achieve, as the author has not, of course, ever had to teach your class. Most books have something useful in them which can be extracted and developed. They can provide examples to thoroughly master something that has already been encountered or questions to extend understanding. Sets of identical texts can be used in collaborative groupings as a means of providing direction, or individually to encourage study skills. Identical texts are particularly useful for group reading procedures in which children all contribute by reading aloud, supported in many cases by the presence of an adult (such as a classroom assistant). Select with care and check the contents carefully before use. Take care not to breach copyright through illegal photocopying; all books contain clear information about what you are allowed to do.

Keynote: To use discretion when selecting texts.

Resources should not dictate the pattern of a lesson

Although sets of text books and other information sources are extremely useful to busy teachers, it is unwise to rely wholly on them to guide your lesson preparation and activities. It is easy to fall into the habit of basing your teaching around the resources rather than using them to enhance and improve pupils' learning. For instance, if standard texts are going to provide helpful information or examples for practice or stimulating ideas, then you should not hesitate to use them. When you are stuck for a fresh approach or simply run out of time to produce lesson plans, a text can be a life-saver, but it is easy to become over-reliant on it at the expense of using your own initiative.

Keynote: To view resources as servants.

Reference books should be used effectively

Every reference book contains some useful information relevant to the subject area in hand; however, it is rare for one book to contain everything that is needed. You have to make a decision about the extent to which you direct pupils' use of the books. You can allow them to skim and scan, use the index and make arbitrary selections of the information that seems useful; this approach tends to lead to large-scale copying from books and the inclusion of inappropriate sections, but encourages greater pupil autonomy. Alternatively, you can pre-select the books and provide more specific directions for use; this approach focuses the learning, but tends to limit pupils' initiative. Try to avoid the situation in which pupils are endlessly scanning books for a snippet of information for long periods of time when, with some specific guidance from you, they could have found the information easily. If you are helping children to develop study skills, there is some merit in leaving pupils to struggle for a time so that they can understand the need to have strategies for cutting through the large amounts of material. Nevertheless, if you want children to use resources skilfully, you will have to teach them how to be selective, use an index, scan text, and extract useful information.

Keynote: To ensure that pupils can access reference material successfully.

Give pupils the basic skills and study skills they need to do the job.

Competence check

- ☐ I have ensured that pupils have acquired the necessary study skills to support their learning
- ☐ I am providing the right kind of support for pupils in their use of library resources and ICT
- ☐ I am being discriminating in my use of printed texts and IT

TMS10 Provide opportunities for pupils to consolidate their knowledge, both in the classroom and through setting well-focused homework, to reinforce and develop what has been learnt

(Section B, 4k, x)

What you need to take account of to meet this standard ...

Use pupils' existing knowledge

Pupils must have some understanding or level of skill which can act as a basis for further development. Ascertaining the extent of children's existing knowledge can be done through talking to them, asking them to complete an elicitation exercise, carrying out a brainstorming session with groups or the class, examining records of previous work. Many teachers try to 'map' children's existing knowledge by using a spider diagram, beginning with a key term and drawing lines from this term to other words and ideas suggested by the children, until a web of interlocking links has been produced. Alternatively, children can be divided into groups to produce their own diagrams (including pictures as appropriate), allowing the teacher to circulate, listen in to the discussions and make note of significant comments. Allowing pupils to map their ideas in this way on a regular basis (say, once every half term) can be used as a way of monitoring their understanding of concepts.

Keynote: To find out how children connect their learning.

Pupils do not have an identical knowledge base

Despite efforts to ensure that all pupils reach an equivalent standard in core learning, the variations in their ability, aptitude and motivation mean that you will always need to spend time reviewing and revising previous learning as a way of ensuring that some basic knowledge can be assumed for the vast majority of the class. By the time children reach the end of their reception class, a considerable variation in their ability and propensity for learning will already be evident. When they leave primary school, it is likely that some children will be struggling to reach Level 2 or 3 in core subject knowledge whereas able ones will be at Level 5 or 6. The majority will, of course, fall between these extremes. These variations mean that however much you differentiate the work, some children will always be at the lower or higher end of the spectrum, even if tasks and activities are tailored for them. It is important to recognise that even if all the children had an individual curriculum, ideally suited to their learning needs, there would still be areas to revise, reinforce and develop. In reality, there will always be some things that children forget, misunderstand and fail to grasp adequately, requiring diligence on your part to detect weaknesses and build on strengths.

Keynote: To take nothing for granted.

Consolidation should follow direct teaching

Some inexperienced or hard-pressed teachers imagine that the use of a well-loved worksheet with lots of problems on it (in mathematics, say) provides the ideal way for children to consolidate their understanding of key concepts. However, unless they are already clear about the principles and ideas associated with the subject matter in hand, the use of a worksheet (or other consolidation techniques) will only result in a lot of mystified and frustrated children asking you the same question repeatedly until you are forced to stop the class and explain things to everyone; which is what you ought to have done in the first place. Learning can, and does, take place through exploratory, investigative and play methods, but you need to be clear in your mind about when the children are working towards a learning outcome and when you are helping them to consolidate their learning. Unless you are clear about the learning intentions for the class, and monitor the pupils' progress carefully, you will not be in a position to know how much consolidation is necessary and when you can press on to the next stage of the learning process. If you underestimate the pupils' grasp of the subject area, you may unwittingly spend too much time consolidating. If you overestimate, you may move on to the next stage before it is appropriate to do so. Regular assessment of pupils' understanding and abilities play a crucial role in determining the right time.

Keynote: To consolidate existing knowledge and understanding.

Some pupils require longer to consolidate than others

It would be wonderful if every pupil progressed at an identical rate. Lesson preparation would be simple; assessments could be carried out in the firm assurance that results would be consistent across the class; consolidation exercises would equally enhance every pupil's grasp of the work, and all the beautifully presented documentation about stages of learning and idealised models of pupil progress would make perfect sense. Unfortunately, learning is not that simple and some children struggle with concepts or mastery while others proceed without a hitch; on other occasions, the children who found certain work easy now find that it is their turn to struggle while others sail through. Such is the nature of learning. The reality of the learning process ensures that smooth and uninterrupted progress exists only in the minds of those who do not have to teach your class! Some children require a lot of support and extra practice; others do not. Some children have to persevere in a way which is unnecessary for the majority. Consolidation is therefore not identical for every child: it may take the form of revising fundamental principles; it may be to refresh children's memory and re-awaken interest; it may act as a spur to further learning. In many cases, consolidation fulfils all these requirements.

Keynote: To allow adequate time for consolidation before introducing new material.

Worksheets should be used constructively

Worksheets (activity sheets) are a useful means of ensuring that a sizeable group of children are engaged on a defined task, thus allowing you to give closer attention to specific children. However, overuse of sheets can lead to tedium and a stale atmosphere as pupils churn through one after another without reflecting on what they are doing or talking about their understanding of the subject area. Although worksheets may serve a useful function in helping to reinforce learning, they have the disadvantage of creating endless amounts of marking and are too often only half-completed or left to gather dust in the bottom of trays. By contrast, the old adage that 'we don't know what we think until we have heard ourselves express it' is a valuable principle governing consolidation. This can be achieved through class or group discussion, written accounts and visual representations. Problem-solving and investigative activities allow pupils to sharpen their newfound understanding and skills on the cutting stone of discovering creative solutions (see also TA6).

Keynote: To use worksheets imaginatively.

Setting and marking homework has time implications

This is true for both pupils and teachers. You have to spend time preparing and explaining the homework; pupils have to complete it; you have to assess or monitor what is done; pupils have to respond to your comments, and so forth. Time factors need to be incorporated into your weekly planning overview and allowance made for the additional demands that will fall on you in managing the process. Even if your school runs a homework club (or similar), time constraints in respect of monitoring and assessing still have to be considered. With the time demands generated through a homework system, it is essential to keep the process transparent and organisationally simple. Elaborate systems cannot be sustained for long as the realities of the working world impinge upon the best-laid plans. All sorts of factors affect the process, such as child absence, timetable alterations, long assemblies and so forth. It is also important to remember that children work at different rates at home in much the same way as they do in school, so homework tasks must take account of these variations. It is unreasonable to set the same task for the whole class which some children can do in ten minutes and others are unable to complete despite many hours of trying. The best homework tasks are those which follow on from the day's lessons; however, it is not always possible or desirable to be rigidly systematic. A satisfactory solution is to balance a regular homework task (such as reading several pages of a set text) with innovative tasks which cover a longer period of time (such as a half term) in which pupils use a variety of study skills to discover more facts about a topic or completion of a booklet containing interesting, open-ended tasks (see also P3).

Keynote: To be realistic about what can be achieved through homework.

Homework tasks should involve parents where possible

Involving parents is not always straightforward. Some parents cannot or do not wish to be involved in their child's education and argue that it is the teacher's job to educate. Pupils who come from homes in which support is not available should not be further disadvantaged by being given homework tasks which are based on the assumption that adult support is available. Nevertheless, the majority of parents like to have some involvement and their assistance with reading tasks (in particular) is important. Many schools have systems in which there is an agreement with parents that they will hear their own children read for a given amount of time each night.

Keynote: To view parental support as desirable but not essential.

There is a difference between managing and assessing homework tasks

Reading several pages of a text each night is usually managed through a 'reading record' in which parents write down the progress their children have made (such as pages read, words encountered, problems arising) and teachers take account of the comments and occasionally add their own. The assessing of homework involves the more demanding task of testing, marking or in some way evaluating the progress that pupils have made as a result of doing it. For instance, if every child has completed a page of English comprehension, you have to spend time going through the passage and reviewing pupils' progress. The work has to be collected in and marked, returned to pupils and issues arising from the task subsequently picked up in class lessons. There is little point in setting a formal homework and failing to assess the resulting product. A lot of exciting homework ideas are impractical due to the heavy assessment demands they generate.

Keynote: To take account of assessment factors when setting homework tasks.

Pupils cannot consolidate what they have not already grasped.

Competence check

☐   I know what children already know
☐   I am distinguishing between teaching and consolidating
☐   Homework is enhancing children's understanding of what they already know

TMS11 Set high expectations for all pupils notwithstanding individual differences, including gender, and cultural and linguistic backgrounds

(Section B, 4k, xiii)

What you need to take account of to meet this standard …

There is a difference between high and unreasonable expectations

All teachers want their pupils to do well. However, in the drive for higher standards it is easy to imagine that there is no end to what can be achieved, with the result that children are pressured and cajoled too much, and made the victims of teachers' anxieties. Genuine achievement should be recognised and acknowledged. Children should, of course, be congratulated and praised when they make genuine progress, and encouraged to do better; this is different from a classroom ethos in which good is never good enough, and children despair of ever satisfying their teacher's insatiable demands for more. As you strive to improve the teaching-and-learning climate, Kyriacou's advice that a relaxed, warm and supportive ethos is an important component (Kyriacou 1991).

Keynote: To have high expectations, not unreasonable ones.

Motivation is a key factor in high achievement

Some pupils have a strong sense of self-motivation; others require strong directing and a degree of coercion. Teachers lives would be much easier if every child was highly motivated, but this is rarely the case. Your job is to develop an atmosphere in which success is celebrated and children become so involved and interested in what they are doing that they will strive for high standards. In the meantime, and for those pupils who are relatively unmotivated or have a passive attitude towards achievement, you need to define your own expectations in such a way that pupils can have no doubt over what is expected. Sometimes this means spelling them out item by item; for instance, see Table 10.

Keynote: To help pupils develop a sense of pride in their work.

It is not easy to define high expectation

Although the principle of high expectations is one that every teacher would espouse, it is not always easy to know what it looks like in respect of individual pupils. You may suspect that children are capable of more, but if they are underachieving, either due to laziness, indifference or lack of motivation, you may not be sure of what they can do if they try hard. Some children are skilled in convincing teachers that they can only achieve a limited amount when in fact they could do

Table 10　Establishing specific expectations for written work

- Write your work in draft form initially without worrying over-much about spelling and punctuation
- Read your work to a trusted friend or the teacher
- Make alterations to your draft as a result of reading it aloud
- With the assistance of a partner if necessary, check spelling, punctuation and grammar
- Show your work to the teacher for a final check
- Write up the work neatly on one side of the paper only, putting your name in the top left hand corner, the date in the top right-hand corner, the title at the top of the page in the centre, then leave two lines of space before you begin writing
- Leave one line of space between each paragraph
- Do not illustrate your work with pictures but add a few touches with coloured pencils (not felt pens) if you wish
- Leave a line of space at the end of your writing and draw a full line across the page
- On the back of the sheet, write a few sentences about how well you think you did this work, and anything you found difficult
- Ask a sensible friend or the teacher to read the final version and tell you what they think about it
- Place the finished work carefully in the 'Finished' box on the teacher's desk

much better. Others lack the confidence and self-esteem to make full use of their abilities. Part of your task as a teacher is to find out the truth by observing closely, encouraging children to aim high and praising genuine effort.

Keynote: To learn what individual pupils are capable of achieving.

Expectations are also subject to differentiation

The five-year-old who manages to write her own name after much perseverance may well deserve congratulating, despite the reversed letters and the sloping script, and regardless of the fact that her classmate learned to write her name when she was three and is now getting on well with joined-up writing. Expectations for the first girl will clearly be different from those for the second. The first girl will need to be encouraged in correct letter formation, whereas the second girl will need to practise hand control before she can write her name without lifting the pencil from the paper. Similarly, expectations for the eleven-year-old boy who has always struggled with spelling cannot be compared with those for his friend who seems to be a walking dictionary! As children grow older, they are increasingly conscious of their own shortcomings and will cease to try if they feel that the teacher is being patronising. If you want the best from your pupils, it is best to be honest with them about their difficulties but to convince them that they can, with your support, achieve something to be proud of.

Keynote: To modify expectations depending upon the individual.

Expectations are not only academic

All teachers are involved with helping to develop the 'whole person', not merely improving academic attainment. One of your tasks as a teacher is to be explicit about what you expect to see in terms of behaviour, attitudes and diligence. Ensuring that pupils are not deprived of their full education on the base of gender, race or culture is a principle that should be enshrined on every teacher's heart. This is not, however, the same as saying that all children should be treated in the same way. Pupils differ in personality, inclination, experience and ability, and wise teachers build on their strengths and try to compensate for their weaknesses. There is little point in producing educated monsters.

Keynote: To expect the best in everything.

Linguistic disadvantage takes many forms

Some children struggle to communicate because of physical factors (such as crooked teeth), emotional factors (such as unhappy experiences with adults), dialects which differ from the majority of pupils (due to moving from another part of the country), home background (and low-level conversations), country of origin (struggling with English as a second language), social pressures (such as the perceived need to speak casually to gain acceptability with other pupils), or psychological factors (such as particular forms of autism). Teachers are sometimes uncertain whether to correct children's speech or encourage them to talk more freely. You need to exercise discretion in such matters: on the one hand to acknowledge and accept diversity; on the other hand, to assist pupils improve their communicative competence through promoting effective speaking and listening. Seek advice from experienced colleagues if uncertain. Make it a rule that you will never tease children because of their dialect or accent.

Keynote: To be aware of communicative weaknesses and ways to make allowance for them.

Many children are caught between cultures

Although we use the term 'culture' to describe particular groups of people, their lifestyles, ideals and (in some cases) religious affiliations, it is important to understand that children live in a multicultural world. Many pupils are caught between the varying expectations of parents, friends, teachers, employers and others in the general community. Although some children may thrive on diversity, it can be difficult for others to know exactly where their loyalties lie and you may observe instances of frustration and depression as a result.

Keynote: To seek ways of celebrating cultural diversity.

We need to be realistic about how much one teacher can cope with

Society has high expectations of schools, but teachers cannot compensate for every family deficiency and personality trait. By helping pupils to learn effectively, and by demonstrating that you value all their endeavours, you can help to provide them with a platform for achieving academic success and establishing their place in the world. The extent to which children make effective use of those opportunities is, however, largely out of your hands, so do not become enmeshed in guilt.

Keynote: To do the best job possible.

Expectations reside in the heart as much as the mind.

Competence check

- ☐   I have established my expectations for pupils' achievement
- ☐   I have communicated those expectations to the children
- ☐   I am taking a positive view of the diversity existing within the class

TMS12 Provide opportunities to develop pupils' wider understanding by relating their learning to real and work-related examples

(Section B, 4k, xiv)

What you need to take account of to meet this standard ...

Reality is a moveable commodity

The things that are unreal today become possibilities tomorrow. The pace of technological advance is so great that almost anything seems possible. The science-fiction comics of a post-war era look tame compared with the amazing progress of recent years. Pupils' approaches to problem-solving situations and their ideas about future innovations have been influenced by the world around them and you must try to keep abreast of the world as they perceive it if you are to understand how children think and feel.

Keynote: To keep pace with events.

Work-related examples must still be appropriate to children's conceptual development

There has been a strong move in recent years towards making the work done in school vocationally orientated, drawing on children's knowledge gained outside school as a means of extending and enhancing their classmates' understanding of the wider world. Many teachers encourage children to bring items relating to that world into school (unless their father is a lion tamer!) and telling their friends about things they have learned. Children watch television programmes and read magazines about differing aspects of work and you may be surprised how much they know if given opportunity to tell. It is also worth remembering that tomorrow's workforce will need to be more adaptable than ever before. Most people will change job at least three or four times. Communication skills, working as a member of a team and individually, use of ICT and the ability to meet strict deadlines will be essential elements of many jobs. You can, and should, assist children in preparing for, and coping with, such a world.

Keynote: To start from the pupils' experience about the world.

The future is unknown but some things never alter

In the 1970s, we were being told that the future would consist of a very short working week and lots of leisure time. It was essential, we were reliably informed, to learn new hobbies, take up sports and find interests with which we could while away the hours. What happened?! You have to be careful that you are not carried away with predicting a world in which ICT dominates lives to such an extent that people will remain in their home, shopping only via the Internet, communicating only via electronic mail and learning solely by means of video-conferencing from the comfort of their own armchair. Some of these trends are already visible and will no doubt continue, but it is important that in our haste to prepare children for such an envisaged world, we do not forget that people are basically gregarious, and that family and community life lies at the heart of a civilised society.

Keynote: To keep a sense of proportion in a changing world.

School is also part of the real world.

Competence check

- ☐ My lessons help pupils to come to terms with reality without losing the innocence of childhood
- ☐ My lessons incorporate a sufficient number of real examples
- ☐ I am making a satisfactory distinction between absolutes and opinions

Chapter 4

Special Educational Needs (SEN1–3)

Special educational needs (SEN) are governed by legislation, notably the Code of Practice (DfEE 1994). There are three principal areas with which you must comply:

SEN1 Familiarity with the Code of Practice and individual education plans (IEPs).
SEN2 Adjusting lesson planning and delivery to take account of children who are not fluent in speaking English.
SEN3 Identifying and responding to very able pupils.

SEN1 Familiarity with using the Code of Practice on the identification and assessment of SEN and keeping records on IEPs for pupils at Stage 2 of the Code and above

(Section B, 4l)

What you need to take account of to meet this standard ...

SEN has first to be identified

Pupils have special educational needs if they are identified as having learning difficulties which are so distinctive from children of a similar age that they call for special provision to be made. The learning difficulty may be due to low academic ability in the case of able-bodied children or a disability which hinders access to, or use of, educational facilities. Thus, disabled children may have the same intellectual ability as their able-bodied peers but make slower progress due to the practicalities of daily living, such as the lack of suitable wheelchair access or an inability to communicate verbally. The earlier that special educational needs can be identified, the more quickly educational provision can be provided. The Code of Practice provides full details of the responsibilities of schools towards children with special educational needs but you need only have a broad grasp of its contents (see FPT, Chapter 5).

Keynote: To be clear about what constitutes special educational needs.

SEN also includes more able pupils

An intelligent and capable child may be struggling to learn for a variety of reasons. This underachievement, once referred to as 'being remedial', is just as significant to the children and parents concerned as those who struggle due to other learning difficulties. Additionally, although there may not be many children in the 'more able' category, you can be fairly certain that there will be at least one case in every class (see SEN3).

Keynote: To be aware of the full range of pupils' abilities.

Every school has to have an SEN policy

Governing bodies of all maintained schools must publish the school's SEN policy and report annually to parents who have children formally identified as needing special support. There is also one person in every school who acts as the special educational needs coordinator (SENCO) who deals with the day-to-day operation of the policy, liaises with colleagues and gives advice where necessary, and coordinates the special provision. All staff are entitled to receive some training about how to deal more effectively with children who have been designated as having special needs. You should ensure that you know who the SENCO is and learn the basic structure of his or her responsibility. In particular, you should be familiar with the mechanism for liaising with the SENCO about your concerns for individual children. Headteachers, in consultation with the SENCO, have to complete forms to indicate how many children are designated as having a special educational need, so accurate information and good communication between teachers and the SENCO about the children is essential.

Keynote: To liaise with the SENCO.

Following the Code of Practice does not, of itself, improve a situation

The Code of Practice and its associated strategies do not provide a blueprint for success. With every good intention and any amount of hard work, some children do not respond as hoped and seem set to struggle for a long time to come. The provision of IEPs can be helpful if there is the time, resourcing and determination to persevere with them and stay on top of the job, but in reality there is no guarantee that they will achieve what is hoped for. Goals have to be established and monitored on the understanding that there are few short-term solutions for deeply entrenched problems. However, it has been shown that active intervention at an early age can, and often does, offset the impact of learning difficulties, providing both child and parents are included in the discussions and establishment of a plan of action. The Code of Practice does at least ensure that pupils do not slip through the net for years, only to be diagnosed towards the end of primary schooling when intervention is much more difficult.

Keynote: To use every means to assist the less able.

Stage 2 of the Code is the point at which an IEP is produced

The IEP should be based on the curriculum that all the other pupils in the class are following, making use of available resources, activities and assessments, and should, as far as possible, form part of the normal classroom setting. It should set out the nature of the learning difficulty, the intended action, how parents can help at home, and some idea of achievement targets. There should be reference in the IEP to monitoring and assessment of the programme, including review arrangements. The review focuses on the effectiveness of the programme and, where possible, involves parents in decisions about whether to draw up a further plan, revert to Stage 1 or, where the situation appears to be deteriorating, call upon external expertise. You will not have to manage these procedures but need to be aware of how IEPs are written and how their effectiveness is monitored.

Keynote: To be familiar with the production and monitoring of IEPs.

Special educational needs in the areas of literacy and numeracy are most urgent

Children may be poor at running, hopeless at art and confused about scientific principles, and it will probably not have a major deleterious effect upon their lives. If, however, they cannot read and write, or deal competently with number bonds, their education will be blighted. This is why most effort is put into ensuring that all possible help is given to children who are failing to make adequate progress in these areas. Schools are now under considerable pressure from the government to improve standards of literacy and numeracy. Inspections of schools also include the work of students and (in particular) NQTs, so there is no hiding place!

Keynote: To concentrate on pupils' literacy.

There are no short-term solutions to special educational needs.

Competence check

☐   I am familiar with the Code of Practice and children with special educational needs

☐   I am liaising with the SENCO

☐   My lessons are taking sufficient account of pupils' needs

SEN2 In lesson planning and delivery, take account of children who are not fluent in English

(Section B, 4a, v)

What you need to take account of to meet this standard ...

Delivery and vocabulary needs to be appropriate

Some inexperienced teachers are prone to speak too quickly or indistinctly, especially when they get excited. If you have pupils for whom English is an additional language (EAL) in the class or group, pay special attention to your diction, pace of speech and phrasing. All children require time to absorb what a teacher says; this is especially true if English is not their native tongue. In particular, you will need to be explicit and careful when using subject-specific vocabulary, casual expressions or colloquialisms. On the other hand, recognise that such pupils will be familiar with the idioms and phrases commonly used by children of their age. Knowing how to explain complex issues using straightforward terminology is a good experience for every teacher.

Keynote: To verbally communicate effectively.

All pupils should be given appropriately challenging work

Children are not unintelligent simply because the first language they speak at home happens to be different from that used by the teachers in school. It is important not to underestimate the ability of EAL children and allocate unsuitable or mundane tasks (see also P3). Careful explanations and close monitoring are particularly important during the first part of the lesson. Relationships between teacher and taught are especially important for children who are not fluent in English as they will often need to confirm and check that what they are doing is correct. Many EAL children will struggle due to the extra communication demands made upon them. If they are placed with a sympathetic and patient child who will help them through the vagaries of the system during the first few weeks in school and given full access to activities in which speech is not wholly essential (such as games and computers) the majority of children quickly settle and fit in. Younger and more vulnerable children will require sympathetic handling, but still need gradual exposure to all aspects of school life. Children with EAL will sometimes require the help of a classroom assistant or language specialist but this does not signify that they are intellectually dull.

Keynote: To recognise the ability and potential of every child.

Some children receive additional support

As part of your planning, you may need to take account of the additional support that a pupil or group of pupils receive. In doing so, check when the support person is available and whether the child receives additional help inside or outside the classroom. If a number of children are classified as coming from New Commonwealth countries, extra support is sometimes provided through a Section 11 teacher. If children go outside the classroom to receive extra support, you will need to take account of the potential distraction when they return and have to be re-integrated into the lesson.

Keynote: To manage the work of additional support staff.

Lesson planning should incorporate speaking and listening activities

Children for whom English is an additional language require regular opportunities to speak and listen, using tape recordings, computer-generated speech or, best of all, other children (see also TMS8). A lot of children are shy or reluctant to speak to adults but may be willing to talk to their peers. It is important to note that some children from other cultures may have been used to having a different relationship with their teachers from the majority of your class. This can lead to over-zealous or unacceptable behaviour for a time until the children have absorbed the class-room norms. You will also need to have a lot of patience and persistence with new pupils who may, on occasions, use their ignorance to exploit the situation.

Keynote: To structure opportunities for speaking.

Pupils who try to speak another language all day can become mentally and emotionally exhausted.

Competence check

- ❑ I am careful in the way that I speak, pronounce words and introduce vocabulary
- ❑ I am ensuring that all children are involved in work appropriate to their ability
- ❑ I am taking sufficient account of pupils' second language needs

SEN3 Identify and respond appropriately to very able pupils

(Section B, 4a, v)

What you need to take account of to meet this standard ...

Able children may be inconspicuous

Not every able child stands out from the rest of the class. Sometimes, the passive child who produces unimaginative written work may prove to have a surprisingly strong grasp of difficult concepts and be capable of solving demanding problems in innovative ways. Some able children are slow of speech and thought, yet far exceed their peers in their understanding of complex issues. Because of large class sizes, it is possible to overlook able children and judge them solely on their visible output. Teare (1997) suggests that able and talented pupils include those who score highly on intelligence tests, but also those who demonstrate outstanding talent in areas as diverse as sporting ability, music, drama and design. He argues that creativity, leadership and organisational qualities, mechanical ingenuity and other human abilities may be signals that a child is able. He also offers a list of criteria by which you can recognise talented and able pupils (see Table 11).

Keynote: To be alert to the existence of special abilities.

Table 11 Characteristics of able and talented children (based on Teare 1997)

- Superior powers of reasoning
- Originality and initiative
- Ability to absorb and classify information
- Detects weaknesses in others, including adults
- Unusually high personal standards
- Absorbed for long periods of time in matters of great personal interest and resents interruption

Able children may be conspicuous

Not all able children are inconspicuous. Some of them are quickly identifiable due to their willingness to answer questions, volunteer for difficult tasks and take responsibility for group activities. Able children are often resourceful, imaginative and hungry for work. They can absorb large amounts of information, search out a variety of facts, complete pages of work, and still come back for more. Many are eager to do well, competent in most areas of the curriculum and popular with their peers. Able children are frequently characterised by their ability to hold sophisticated conversations with adults and incorporate their experiences from outside school into their daily work.

Keynote: To celebrate the talent and enthusiasm of able pupils.

Able children may be restless spirits

All children can be restless at times, but some of the very able children may find it difficult to settle to regular work. Such children wander about the room, poking into the library, commenting on what might appear to be trivial bits of knowledge that they have gleaned from different sources. Sometimes they prefer to work alone and spend excessive amounts of time on a narrowly focused activity in order to satisfy their thirst for mental engagement. You may be tempted (quite understand-ably) to give these non-conformists some straightforward tasks to keep them tied down; however, if you can present them with a variety of problem-solving tasks which hold their interest and stretch their intellects, you will soon find out whether the child is truly able or just lacking the ability to concentrate.

Keynote: To focus intellectual energy into purposeful activities.

Able children need to be valued

Although they excel in some aspects of academic work, very able children are as diverse as other groups of children in terms of how good their aptitude for sport, their preferences, hobbies and interests. Able children may be emotionally imma-ture or quite sophisticated. Whatever their personal characteristics, you should treat them in a way that is appropriate to their ages and not as alien beings who inhabit the school planet! Able children also need encouragement and praise. It is surprisingly easy to 'let them get on with it' or to minimise their achievements by saying, in effect, that as they have a good brain they do not deserve credit for anything. Part of your task is to value effort and achievement for every child at every level.

Keynote: To enthuse about all achievement.

Extreme ability may gain a child popularity or scorn

Many able children are popular with their peers, especially if they are willing to share their expertise and be helpful during lessons. However, if able children are perceived as slightly odd or are socially immature, they may attract unwelcome attention, disregard or bullying. It has been known for able children to under-achieve as a means of maintaining friendships which they might otherwise have forfeited. It is part of your responsibility to develop a culture of learning with your pupils, such that achievement and the application of mental ability of other skills are seen as positive attributes rather than oddities. Children have to be shown that serious work and achievement can be just as much fun as messing about with trivial activities.

Keynote: To foster a work culture.

Ability goes beyond the school curriculum

Some children are expert in areas not covered by the curriculum, such as hobbies developed at home, interests shared with a parent or a passion that has grown through the years. In addition, there are many children who, though they never excel academically, are exceptional in terms of their caring ways, sincerity, endeavour and friendly disposition. If you show enthusiasm about the things that children value, and make a point of allowing them to share their achievements with others, you will discover their many hidden talents. Once you have demonstrated to your pupils that effort, diligence and perseverance in situations outside the school curriculum are also worth celebrating, success quickly becomes infectious.

Keynote: To celebrate every form of determined effort.

There should be no hidden treasures lying undiscovered in pupils.

Competence check

- ☐ I have identified pupils with special abilities
- ☐ I have made adequate provision for their needs in my planning
- ☐ I am developing a culture of success among my pupils

Chapter 5

Assessment (A1–7)

The role of assessment in learning has been highlighted over recent years. You need to demonstrate your competence in seven key areas:

A1 Assessing pupils' achievements as a means of improving planning and teaching.
A2 Marking and monitoring progress.
A3 Recording pupils' progress as a means of improving their learning.
A4 Assessing pupils against attainment targets.
A5 Familiarity with level descriptions and end-of-key-stage descriptions.
A6 Using different kinds of assessment appropriately.
A7 Using assessment data to establish learning targets for pupils.

A1 Assess how well learning objectives have been achieved and use this assessment to improve planning and specific aspects of teaching

(Section B, 4c and Section C, a)

What you need to take account of to meet this standard ...

Assessments can be random or specific

The majority of teacher assessments are gained randomly as they notice pupils' behaviour and attitudes, hear them making comments about the work, see the written outputs they produce and pick up snippets of other relevant information. Some assessments are more structured, especially information gained through question and answer, responses to tasks, and discussion groups. Some assessments are highly structured when information about pupils' learning is gained through test conditions and formal marking criteria.

Keynote: To be aware of different assessment opportunities.

The best assessments influence planning

Assessment of pupils' progress is not merely to provide information to put on a record card or in a school report but to assist in lesson preparation. There are three aspects of assessment that you can use: (i) specific errors made by pupils in their answers to questions or written work which indicate misunderstanding; (ii) incorrect answers made during reinforcement activities which show that basic concepts need revising; (iii) pupils' overall grasp of skills and concepts which provide evidence that it is time to introduce more advanced work. The third of these is particularly important as assessment is sometimes viewed as ways of discovering pupil failings rather than pupil successes. Consequently, assessment has acquired a negative image which it hardly deserves. Once you see assessment as a means of enhancing your teaching and learning, you will never be short of material for future lessons.

Keynote: To use assessment constructively.

Learning objectives and learning outcomes may differ

However carefully you design your lessons, you cannot guarantee that the children will learn what you intend them to, or even that you will discover what they have learned. Teaching and learning rarely follows a simple progression from planning to teaching to outcomes to assessment. Because the children were all listening to you at the same time and engaged on identical or similar tasks, it does not mean that they have learned the same things. As it is impossible to assess every child during every session, it is useful to select a few 'target' children and examine the evidence for their learning more closely to act as a yardstick for the class as a whole. You can change the children that you target from time to time to get a more complete picture. The more specific you can be about what you hope the children learn (or begin to learn) the more you will be able to evaluate what is happening and use the assessment information gained to plan future lessons, but it would be a mistake to believe that it is a smooth operation.

Keynote: To monitor learning outcomes.

Assessment does not always improve learning

You can spend a lot of time pouring over samples of children's work, talking to them about what they should have learned and applying a battery of formal tests, but they will not of themselves make a great deal of difference unless you scrutinise the evidence and think through the implications for your own lesson planning. Some inexperienced teachers spend precious time compiling fancy lists of assessment results which, though they may look very impressive, have a limited impact on their classroom performance or the way they organise learning. Unless assessment and recording has a positive impact on teaching effectiveness, you may as well save yourself the trouble.

Keynote: To spend assessment time wisely.

Pupils can give helpful information

Take note of what the children say about your lessons. Watch how enthusiastic they are to do more of the same. Listen for their comments as they leave the room. Read their body language. If possible, find out directly through casual questioning of some key pupils how they perceived the lesson and what they made of it. The best lessons may not always be the most popular with pupils, but they are usually characterised by a notable increase in children's verbal responsiveness.

Keynote: To encourage self-assessment.

> Effective assessment facilitates learning.

Competence check

- ☐ My lesson evaluation incorporates assessment of learning objectives
- ☐ I am using a variety of sources to gain an overall impression of lesson success
- ☐ I am using information from one lesson to guide my detailed planning for future lessons

A2 Mark and monitor pupils' assigned classwork and homework, provide constructive oral and written feedback and set targets for pupils' progress

(Section C, b)

What you need to take account of to meet this standard ...

Marking has time and practical implications

Marking is usually a slow business if carried out thoroughly (see P3 and TMS10). For instance, if you have 30 Year 6 essays to mark at home, it will take you at least four hours to complete. Similarly, marking 60 pages of mathematical computations is an exhausting task. Some work requires no more than a cursory glance to ensure completion. Some can be marked by pupils themselves. Other work needs to be taken and marked away from the classroom. The majority of work should, ideally, be marked during the lesson with the pupils present or as soon after the teaching event as possible. You have to decide whether the time taken in marking is justified in terms of the value to children's learning.

Keynote: To clarify the purpose of marking.

Decide whether written or oral feedback is best

A lot of monitoring can be undertaken through speaking to the pupils concerned and providing constructive suggestions, asking searching (but non-threatening) questions and involving other children in providing ideas and suggestions about appropriate methods or solutions. Written feedback is far more time consuming and, with the best will in the world, usually consists of only a few words. Although children like to see comments such as 'Well done, you have worked hard' on their work, these are more to encourage than to assess the quality. Children will make most progress when they take careful note of your feedback and are encouraged by your response to persevere. A lot of red pen across the page damages pupils' self-esteem.

Keynote: To provide appropriate feedback.

Involve the pupils in setting targets

The expression 'target setting' can invoke a lot of anxiety amongst teachers. However, it is simply a way of helping pupils to move from their current position of understanding and capability to a more secure or advanced one. Most targets can be set by talking to the pupils concerned and pointing out how things might be improved. Many children are acutely aware of the need for improvement and are anxious to do so. They may be less clear about the standard they need to reach and strategies for achieving it. Part of your role as a teacher is to provide guidance in helping them do so (see Pascal and Bertram 1997 for early years case studies in improvement). It may be appropriate to encourage children to keep their own records of progress by providing them with a list of 'I can do …' items relevant to the topic or subject area that they can tick for themselves (Clemson and Clemson 1996).

Keynote: To involve pupils in their learning.

Homework should not become burdensome

With the increased attention paid to the importance of homework in raising standards, it is tempting to place too much emphasis upon it and create something of a monster that absorbs too much of your time and attention, and makes too many demands upon young children (see also P3 and TMS10). Homework should be easy to administer and monitor. Where possible, pupils and parents should take the major responsibility for the administration (such as marking reading records); your task is to incorporate elements of the work into mainstream classwork. If you find that setting and marking homework detracts from your principal responsibilities for the daily teaching-and-learning programme, you need to reduce its priority rating.

Keynote: To use homework to support teaching and learning.

Teachers are not marking machines.

Competence check

☐   I am following the school's and class teacher's marking policy
☐   I am monitoring and marking work in a way that assists pupils' learning
☐   I am using information from monitoring and marking to help shape my lesson planning

A3   Assess and record each pupil's progress systematically, using focused observation, questioning, testing and marking

(Section C, c)

Use these records effectively to:

1   check that pupils have understood and completed the work set;
2   monitor strengths and weaknesses and use the information gained as a basis for purposeful intervention in pupils' learning;
3   inform planning;
4   check that pupils continue to make demonstrable progress in their acquisition of the knowledge, skills and understanding of the subject.

What you need to take account of to meet this standard ...

Assessing and recording for every pupil is a major task

The description contained within this standard may lead teachers to attempt the impossible task of providing individual curricula for every pupil. Even experienced teachers find it difficult to keep pace with every pupil's progress in each key area of the curriculum. Maintaining records which accurately reflect children's understanding, strengths and weaknesses is based on the assumption that all progress is quantifiable and has led to teachers wasting a considerable amount of time in endlessly ticking, colouring and annotating records and lists. It is only worth filling in a record if it is useful in one of two ways: either it gives information to help parents understand their children's progress or it helps you to reflect more purposefully on ways of improving learning (see FPT, Chapter 10).

Keynote: To maintain essential records.

There must be valid and reliable methods of testing

Any form of test must take account of two things: its validity and its reliability. A test has to be valid in that the results are a true reflection of a pupil's knowledge, understanding or skill level in an area of learning. For instance, if you are testing ten-year-olds' ability to read and interpret instructions, it would be valid to use a sample of writing based on (say) a design and technology project on which the class had recently been engaged, but invalid to use text from a book on quantum mechanics, about which the pupils were completely unfamiliar. Similarly, it would be valid to test pupils' understanding of number bonds if they were presented in a conventional form (base-10), but invalid if children were suddenly given sums in base-5! The extent of a test's reliability can be found in whether the results can be replicated through further, similar tests. For instance, some new school entrants are coached by parents just prior to starting school and may thereby achieve an inflated score in their baseline assessment (see below); if, after the lapse of ten days or so, the same test yielded markedly different results, we might suspect that the test was unreliable for the trained group of children, though reliable for the other entrants. Reliability, then, has to take account of the conditions under which the test is given and the circumstances influencing the outcome. Thus, if children have to take an examination in an unfamiliar place with teachers they have never met, their results may not reflect their ability due to their insecurity; in such a case, we would probably feel justified in claiming that the results were unreliable even if the test itself was valid.

Keynote: To take account of validity and reliability of tests.

Focused observation requires planning

In a busy primary classroom, it is normally impossible to spend any length of time observing a single pupil. To do so requires particular forms of planning: giving the class a task which will keep pupils busily occupied to minimise demands upon yourself; using a classroom assistant or fellow teacher to take the major responsibility for the class while you record your judgements; organising lessons in such a way that the target children are engaged in tasks which provide the sort of information you are looking for. It is not possible to observe everything at once and it is sensible to select two or three specific areas of learning or behaviour for special attention. For instance, you might be interested in seeing how independently children work, the length of their attention span, their application to the task or their use of equipment. You may, on the other hand, wish to note how often they interrupt others, support their partners, offer verbal contributions or write down ideas. As part of any focused observation, you will also want to ask fundamental questions about the quality of work produced by paying attention to whether the task was well matched to the child and the impact of the organisation for learning (Wragg 1994).

Keynote: To organise for observing.

Records are only a snapshot in time

However rapidly you complete a record sheet after assessing progress, it will always be out of date. Young children, in particular, will make sudden spurts in their learning which confound your earlier assessments; others will appear to have grasped something, only for you to find that they did not understand it so well after all. It is simply not possible for teachers to constantly update record cards, so they will inevitably show an incomplete picture. Most up-to-date records of pupils' progress have to be kept in your head until the important points can be written down.

Keynote: To keep records in perspective.

Records of Achievement are valuable sources of information

Since the introduction of the National Curriculum, many schools have introduced a system of files or folders in which aspects of a pupil's work, skills, abilities and personal qualities are acknowledged. Primary schools often include a portfolio of each child's work, in which samples from different areas of the curriculum are included. Mitchell and Koshy (1995) suggest that a good Record of Achievement will recognise that children learn at different speeds and that their abilities and development are not fixed. It helps children to reflect carefully about the quality of their work as they select, with teacher support, samples to be included in the folder. A concentration of positive achievements can also be a spur to self-confidence and success. If you are involved in helping children to select from their repertoire for inclusion in the folder, you may be surprised at some of their choices (which will be different from your own). The process of selection does give opportunity for you to talk to the children about their work and discuss standards. Any work included in the folder should contain the date of completion and some brief details concerning the level of support the child received (see FPT, Chapter 10).

Keynote: To use Records of Achievement as a spur to progress.

> Even if you had a class of one, you could never know everything there was to know about the child.

Competence check

☐ My records provide useful and usable information about the progress of individuals

☐ I have based my decisions about progress on a range of sources

☐ I have a clearer understanding of individual pupils' knowledge and understanding after assessing and recording than I did before

A4 Recognise the level at which a pupil is achieving and assess them consistently against attainment targets where applicable, if necessary with guidance from an experienced teacher

(Section C, g)

What you need to take account of to meet this standard ...

Attainment targets are guides to achievement

The eight level descriptions describe the types and range of performance that pupils working at a particular level should characteristically demonstrate. From time to time it is a useful exercise to practise matching samples of children's work in mathematics, English and science with the appropriate National Curriculum descriptors to get a feel for the standards at different levels. Although attainment targets provide a useful measure of pupils' progress, they are neither infallible nor absolute. They offer one means of assessing achievement by providing a 'best fit' for pupil attainment. They should not be dismissed as irrelevant or elevated beyond their usefulness. Unfortunately, because they have assumed such a high profile in gauging teaching effectiveness and reporting to parents, they tend to be thought of as the final word rather than one indicator among many.

Keynote: To use levels of achievement as a rough guide to pupils' progress.

There are national compulsory tests and tasks during primary schooling

Tests and tasks are given to all children at the end of Key Stages 1 and 2. Tests are in areas where it is possible to give a numerical score; tasks require teacher assessment and moderation by teachers in different schools. The two Standard Assessment Tasks (SATs) cover the following areas:

• Year 2 children: reading, writing (including handwriting), spelling and mathematics;
• Year 6 children: reading, writing (including handwriting), spelling, mathematics, mental arithmetic and science.

Keynote: To be aware of national requirements.

SATs form the heart of formal assessment

The SATs are the most notable example of determining attainment levels. Headteachers receive details of the tasks a few weeks in advance of the time they have to be taken but are not allowed to open them until shortly before they are administered. Teachers of Year 2 usually have to make a considerable effort to organise the tests, normally with the help of another teacher (who may be brought in for this purpose). Once the tests have been completed, some of the answers can be marked using an optical reader; others require marking according to set criteria. The accumulated marks for the different sections of the SATs are collated (sometimes using computer software) and a final level of attainment for mathematics and English is determined. The process is not intended to disrupt the children's education but there are inevitably some undesirable consequences, including preparing children for the tests by 'cramming' and getting children back into a routine once the tests are over. Teachers are also left with the arduous job of transferring the SATs results into a format which parents can understand. Year 6 teachers follow a similar procedure to those of Year 2 pupils, but in their case the tests include science, and the completed test papers are sent away for external marking.

Keynote: To become familiar with procedures for SATs.

Teachers have to provide their own assessments of pupils

Teachers are responsible for assessing pupils' progress through the normal procedures of setting and evaluating work from day to day, together with any in-school tests that may be used to provide a clearer picture of children's progress. Teacher assessments are required for some areas of English, mathematics and science in addition to the formal SATs testing. Key Stage 2 assessments at Levels 1 and 2 are made by the teacher. Teachers of pupils in Years 2 and 6 have to provide their own evidence for levels of attainment, based on comparing pupils' work with that of children of similar age elsewhere by using published guides containing performance descriptions (SCAA 1995). Teachers from the different schools in a locality also bring along samples of work to the forum as a means of monitoring consistency of judgement for samples of English work (especially writing). In practice, teachers tend to wait until the SATs results are available before finally committing themselves to grades for their children. Teacher assessment levels for any one child are frequently identical to the SATs result.

Keynote: To have suitable evidence to carry out teacher assessments.

Levels of achievement are used to compare the success of schools

It is important for you to understand that although the children's progress is of immediate concern to you, there is a wider agenda involving governors, inspectors, local authorities and national education bodies (such as the Qualifications and Curriculum Authority (QCA)) in which results are used to determine the school's success. If results do not meet expectations, headteachers and governors may find themselves criticised by inspectors and, if things do not improve, the school may be placed under close scrutiny until it improves.

Keynote: To be part of a collaborative effort in raising standards.

> Assessment through testing forms an integral part of school life.

Competence check

☐ I am familiar with the appropriate attainment targets
☐ I have concentrated my efforts on ensuring that pupils have a firm grasp of core subjects areas
☐ I have taken advice from a more experienced teacher about measuring attainment

A5 Understand the expected demands of pupils in relation to each relevant level description or end-of-key-stage description, where applicable

(Section C, e)

What you need to take account of to meet this standard ...

Level descriptions should not dominate curriculum planning and assessment

It is surprisingly easy to orientate your teaching in such a way that you 'teach to the test' by training children in an unimaginative way rather than allowing them to explore learning and gain important experience about failure and disappointment, giving them the opportunity to modify or redesign particular approaches, and follow instinctive lines of enquiry that lead to learning outcomes which are different from the ones that you originally intended. It is useful to keep your eye on level descriptions but not to allow them to dictate everything you want children to learn.

Keynote: To distinguish between education and training.

End-of-key-stage descriptions only apply to certain subjects

Art, music and PE are assessed using end-of-key-stage descriptions which indicate the type and range of performance that the majority of pupils should characteristically demonstrate by the end of that key stage, assuming that they have been taught the necessary programmes of study. The eight level descriptions are not used for these three subjects.

Keynote: To become familiar with end-of-key-stage descriptions.

Literacy permeates every curriculum area

The ability to read and write is important regardless of the subject being studied. Pupils need to have a firm grasp of literacy and develop the ability to express themselves orally if they are to extend their learning. You need to do all that you can to encourage children to develop effective study skills (such as the use of an index, a dictionary and a database) and communication skills (such as the ability to summarise findings, explain things to other pupils, tell a friend how something is done) if they are to make the most of their opportunities. In particular, most good readers are potentially high achievers; whereas poor readers, regardless of how hard you try to motivate them, will tend to underachieve, even in those areas of learning which do not require strong reading ability (see P5 and TMS9).

Keynote: To enhance standards of literacy.

Attainment Target 1 makes particular demands of pupils and teachers

The AT1 for English, mathematics and science in the National Curriculum involves Speaking and Listening, Using and Applying Mathematics and Experimental and Investigative Science, respectively. These areas of the curriculum are quite demanding for teachers to plan as they require a variety of teaching methods to be employed, including, for example, interactive class or group discussion to facilitate speaking and listening skills, and mathematical investigations based on relevant situations. Typically, lessons can be based on the mathematics of building a school extension, plans for the establishment of a new play area, the correct size of hat brim to ensure protection from the effects of the sun, repositioning the classroom furniture to allow for safe access. Science experiments should allow for collaborative planning, design, testing and recording of results in a variety of ways. Lessons in these curriculum areas give you clear insights into children's grasp of skills and concepts.

Keynote: To tackle the curriculum in AT1 with determination.

Level descriptions are only a general guide to a pupil's ability and potential.

Competence check

☐   I am familiar with the appropriate level descriptions and end-of-key-stage descriptions

☐   I have not allowed level descriptions to dominate my planning

☐   My lesson planning includes opportunities for pupils in AT1

A6 Use different kinds of assessment appropriately for different purposes, including National Curriculum and other standardised tests, and baseline assessment where relevant

(Section C, i)

What you need to take account of to meet this standard ...

Pupils are assessed on entering school

All pupils aged four or five years, both full and part-time, have to be assessed on admittance to a primary school, unless they are placed in a designated nursery class (QCA 1997). Every baseline assessment scheme (QCA 1998) has to cover aspects of language and literacy, mathematics, and personal and social development as specified in the 'desirable outcomes' (SCAA 1997; Table 12). Included in the assessment must be one or more quantitative results capable of being used for later 'value-added' analyses (see below). Pupils are assessed by the class teacher within the first half term using information from playgroup leaders, nursery teachers and parents wherever possible about the children's strengths, achievements (or lack of them), and placed in a category level using a 'best fit' approach. In liaison with parents, targets are set for future progress and some arrangements made for future review of progress. Many baseline assessment schemes include details about children's pre-school attendance, free school meal entitlement, ethnic background and special educational needs (Lindsay and Desforges 1998). Assessments must be carried out within the first seven weeks of a child entering school and look certain to place heavy time demands upon reception class teachers.

Keynote: To have a clear idea about pupils' current capability.

Table 12 Desirable outcomes for children's learning (SCAA 1997)

- Personal and social development
- Language and literacy
- Mathematics
- Knowledge and understanding of the world
- Physical development
- Creative development

Baseline assessments provide a marker for future progress

Subsequent progress in reading and number at the end of Key Stage 1 (when the child is aged about seven years) is compared with the baseline assessment. The difference between the scores is known as 'value-added' to indicate the difference that the early years of schooling has made to the child's attainment (Tymms 1996). Schools are expected to ensure that there has been substantial progress during the intervening time. It is not only helpful to know children's current attainment but the rate at which they seem to be improving. The validity of this type of comparison has been called into question. There are also optional tests for Years 3, 4 and 5 available to schools who want to monitor pupils' progress more closely. Schools are not obliged to disclose these results to parents, though some elect to do so. One reason for carrying out baseline assessments is to try to ensure that schools with intakes of low achievers are not unfairly disadvantaged compared with their capable neighbours. It is obvious that children who enter school already well advanced in their academic work are likely to achieve higher results in their Key Stage 1 assessments by the time they are seven. However, with a baseline assessment available, the extent of each child's progress can (it is claimed) be calculated. One advantage of this approach to determining pupils' achievement is that it allows schools with weaker Key Stage 1 SATs results to demonstrate that pupils have made some progress, albeit from a lower starting point, compared with schools in which children come from more advantaged backgrounds. One reason why it is important for schools to show that pupils are progressing is that the 'value-added' element provides a measure of teaching effectiveness (see Table 13).

Keynote: To measure the extent of pupils' progress.

Table 13 An example of a baseline assessment schema

1 Qualitative statements in the form of a profile are provided by a nursery or reception teacher when the child starts school, together with information from parents (sometimes gained through home visits by teachers from the receiving schools)

2 The reception teacher makes a 'best fit' for the child's present achievements using a graded series of descriptors in the areas of Social and emotional development/ Language/ Mathematics

3 Future achievements are compared with the baseline assessment profile to determine the children's progress in number and reading (in particular)

Tests and tasks take time

The tests and tasks are held during the summer term for seven-year-olds, usually spread over several days to avoid undue fatigue. Tests for eleven-year-olds normally take place on set days during May. Tests are sent away for external marking. The SATs for Year 2 children are not intended to take more than three hours in total, and around five hours for Year 6 children. It is important to remember that these are the times that the children actually spend in carrying out the tests and tasks. Teachers have to commit additional time in understanding the requirements, sorting out the tasks, organising for the tests to take place and other administrative tasks. If children are absent on the day of the test, separate arrangements need to be made for them to sit it. This in itself causes more work and organisation. The national assessment tests are marked externally. Results are returned to schools in time for their annual reports to parents in which test results have to be disclosed.

Keynote: To take account of tasks and tests in organising teaching.

There are levels of achievement for SATs

Most children in Year 2 should reach at least Level 2 in the tests. Most children in Year 6 should reach at least Level 4. The government is trying to increase the percentage of children achieving these grades and insisting that schools set increasingly higher targets. Very able pupils at the end of Key Stage 1 can be entered for the Key Stage 2, Level 4 tests in reading, writing or mathematics. To allow for variations in children's ages, the raw scores in English reading and spelling tests and the mathematics test at Key Stages 1 and 2 will all be adjusted by teachers to give scores which more fairly reflect attainment by making allowance for the considerable differences that may be found in children depending on their date of birth. A separate test for mental arithmetic, lasting some 20 to 30 minutes is now part of the statutory assessment

Keynote: To understand the expectations for levels of achievement.

Parents are entitled to information about their child's level of attainment

Following statutory assessments, parents have a right to request written information about their child's level of attainment in each attainment target of the core subjects on the National Curriculum 1–8 scale. Headteachers are obliged to provide this information within three weeks (see Table 14 as an example of how a report is structured).

Keynote: To be aware of parental rights.

Assessment results follow the child from school to school

Some children transfer at age seven or eight years to a different school. The sending school has to supply the receiving school with the child's most recent and all previous statutory assessment results in English, mathematics and science. Similarly, when pupils transfer from primary to secondary school, their Key Stage 2 test results will accompany them.

Keynote: To facilitate continuity of assessment.

Table 14   End of Key Stage 1 assessment results: report to parents

Levels of attainment are provided in the following subject areas:

English
• Teacher assessment results in Speaking and Listening/Reading/Writing
• Task and test results in reading task/reading comprehension test/writing task/spelling test

Mathematics
• Teacher assessment result
• Task and test results

Science
• Teacher assessment result
• There are no tasks or tests in science at Key Stage 1

Teachers are under pressure during the time of SATs

Although teachers are becoming more used to managing national tests and tasks, they involve a lot of effort and close cooperation between the teachers involved and the headteacher. Gipps, Brown and McAllister (1995) found that 25 out of 31 school headteachers reported increased levels of stress during the administration of the SATs. Schools with the highest stress levels were those in which there had been a considerable amount of reorganisation and disruption to accommodate the tests. Teachers' anxiety was also found to be due to the high profile that the assessments received and, from Key Stage 1 staff, the need formally to label young children. If you are a student teacher, you need to be aware of the increased pressure on staff during the SATs season and the possible changes to the normal teaching programme which may accompany it. If you are placed with a Year 2 or Year 6 class during their assessment period, you will have to demonstrate flexibility and offer your full support to the teachers involved, regardless of the imposition it makes on your teaching programme. If you are a new teacher, it is unlikely that you will be asked to take a Year 2 or 6 class during your first year, unless you are in a village school with several year groups in the same class.

Keynote: To be especially cooperative during a period of formal assessment.

Assessment tests and tasks should follow the work, not the other way round.

Competence check

☐   I am broadly familiar with the composition of baseline assessments
☐   I understand the significance of tasks and tests at the end of key stages
☐   I am familiar with the requirements for teacher assessments

A7 Understand and know how national, local, comparative and school data, including National Curriculum test data, can be used to set clear targets for pupils' achievement

(Section C, h)

What you need to take account of to meet this standard ...

A wide range of data can be used in target setting

To set appropriate targets for pupils, it is essential to use all available information (OFSTED/DfEE 1996), although it takes time to trawl through past records, talk to staff and examine current records, in addition to using more immediate assessment tasks and strategies to gain an up-to-date picture. It is important to evaluate a pupil's achievements by reference to a wide range of data to gain an accurate profile of ability and potential (see Figure 7). A child may be top of the class but still underachieving. Another child may be in the middle range of achievements for the class, but doing well or poorly by contrast with similar groups of the same age elsewhere. You have to make a professional judgement about what an individual might achieve, while being sensitive to what realistically can be achieved.

Keynote: To use data constructively.

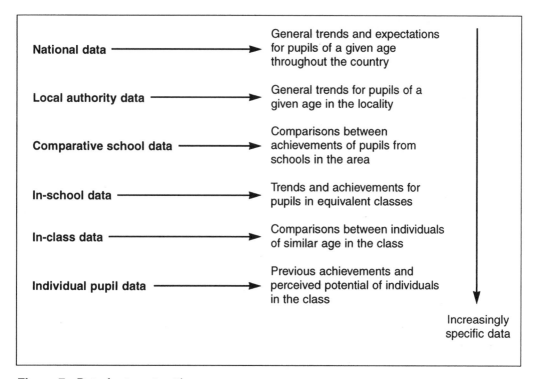

National data	General trends and expectations for pupils of a given age throughout the country
Local authority data	General trends for pupils of a given age in the locality
Comparative school data	Comparisons between achievements of pupils from schools in the area
In-school data	Trends and achievements for pupils in equivalent classes
In-class data	Comparisons between individuals of similar age in the class
Individual pupil data	Previous achievements and perceived potential of individuals in the class

Increasingly specific data

Figure 7 Data for target setting

The SATs results of individual children are confidential

The national tests are an attempt to allow comparisons between the performance of different schools. Schools are obliged to print a summary of their year's SATs results in their brochure for parents, so that they are kept fully informed of the overall picture. Results are also published in newspapers. However, only the parents or guardians of individual children are entitled to receive the specific information pertaining to their children. You should be careful not to share specific test scores with anyone who does not have a direct professional interest in them. Parents are entitled to see their children's completed task and test papers.

Keynote: To respect confidentiality.

Differences between teacher assessment and test results may have to be explained

In reports to parents, teachers have to provide a brief comment about what the assessment levels indicate about a child's progress. If there are variations between the teacher assessments and results from tasks and tests, some explanation may be needed to justify the differences. For instance, teachers may need to explain that their own assessments are based on a longer-term perspective than the external ones, which provide only a snapshot of a child's understanding at a given time and place.

Keynote: To have appropriate evidence to support teacher assessments.

SATs results do not tell the whole story

Any formal assessment task has to take account of at least six factors. First, some children are frightened by a formal situation and may underachieve due to anxiety. Second, however carefully a test is designed, it will be interpreted differently by different pupils. Third, cultural norms and preferences affect the way in which pupils respond to questions. Fourth, some children have English as an additional language or have poor language skills which may hinder their ability to work rapidly and efficiently. Fifth, tests demand a concentration span of which some pupils are incapable. Sixth, some pupils do not begin their academic growth until they are older and therefore fail to register a satisfactory SATs result in Key Stage 1. Broadfoot (1996) notes that children's achievements are often affected by the learning context itself. Despite the great care that is taken by the QCA to produce tests and tasks that are both valid and reliable, SATs are subject to the same sort of limitations as other tests and should be used alongside your knowledge of the individual needs and potential of the child concerned (Drummond 1993).

Keynote: To put SATs results into perspective.

Schools have to keep samples of work of equivalent standard to the different National Curriculum levels of attainment

Many schools have a large book with samples of children's work in core subjects to indicate the sort of work which is equivalent to a particular standard. Class teachers will have samples of children's work with an indication of the conditions under which the work was carried out and the teachers' assessment of its quality.

Keynote: To examine typical samples of children's work at different levels.

Every piece of work has a history.

Competence check

- ☐ I am aware of the need to set appropriate targets for learning
- ☐ I understand that a profile of a child's achievements relies both on the teacher's assessment and the standard tasks and tests
- ☐ I have taken test and task results into account when planning lessons and series of lessons

Chapter 6

Reporting (R1)

Assessment, recording and reporting to parents tend to be inter-related. However, there is one specific standard relating solely to reporting:

R1 Knowing how to prepare and present informative reports to parents.

R1 Familiarity with the statutory assessment and reporting and knowing how to prepare and present informative reports to parents

(Section C, d)

What you need to take account of to meet this standard ...

Most schools actively encourage parents to make contributions to school development

Gone are the days when schools used to have a sign saying 'No parents past this point'. In today's consumer climate and with the extent of accountability demanded of headteachers and governors, parents are represented through the appointment of at least one parent governor and a variety of other means. For instance, some schools canvass parents before taking important decisions; others set up open forums or take samples of parental opinion. Inspectors take careful note of the seriousness with which schools treat parental opinion. A school may face severe criticism if it has taken insufficient account of parents' views. Parents are one of the most powerful voices in education. You should take every opportunity to develop a friendly, professional relationship with them (see FPT, Chapter 3).

Keynote: To value parental contributions to learning.

Schools are not always willing or able to involve students in the reporting process

If you are still training, you may find that some teachers are quite nervous about allowing you to have access to parents for fear that you might say or do something to the detriment of the class or school. Other teachers will only allow more experienced students to have contact with parents. Many teachers allow informal contact but draw the line at anything formal. Very few schools allow students to write formal comments about pupils to send to parents, though the teacher responsible for the class or group will value receiving some information from you about pupils' progress that can be incorporated into the record system for future use. You may need to arrange with your mentor an opportunity to offer your written comments to a 'surrogate' parent (perhaps another teacher who agrees to help) and receive feedback on their value.

Keynote: To practise writing reports.

Parents are entitled to a lot of information about their child's progress

The parents of primary school leavers receive a report containing several pages of statistical information, including all the information gained through the national assessments at Key Stages 1 and 2 in core subjects, together with (in the majority of cases) a comment from a teacher or teachers on each subject: English, mathematics, science, history, geography, design and technology, information and communication technology, art, music and PE. Although parents will look at the statistical information, it is likely that they will be particularly interested in the nature of the teachers' comments, especially concerning their child's attitude, achievements, potential and non-academic strengths (see Figure 8). All the quantitative results from tests and tasks are expressed as levels on a common scale from 1 to 8; similarly, teacher assessments are placed within the same range of levels. Reports will also include a summary of school results for the year and national results from the previous year, allowing parents to compare broadly the progress of their children against others of the same age in the school and across the country. Not all parents realise that test results are only one measure of ability and that overall standards, particularly in very small schools, are bound to vary from year to year.

Keynote: To be familiar with parental entitlements.

All written comments will be interpreted by the parents

Teachers who write anything which is seen by parents have to make certain that they check the accuracy of its contents, the validity of its claims and the correctness of the syntax and spelling. Ambiguity can create unnecessary alarm and, in some cases, hostility from parents who see your remarks as a personal affront. Headteachers are usually explicit about the kind of written information they wish

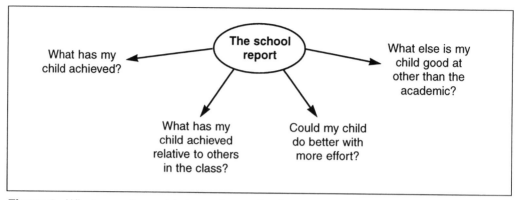

Figure 8   What parents want to know from school reports

to be included (if any), so make every effort to conform to the agreed pattern. In addition to bland comments about progress, try to include a positive remark about the child's attitude, contributions to the life of the class and school, and potential. While needing full information about their children's academic progress, a parent of a less able child, in particular, needs to feel that there is hope for their offspring's future.

Keynote: To write reports with the readers in mind.

> Reports are read eagerly by parents.

Competence check

☐   I understand parents' entitlements concerning written information
☐   I know that both national assessments and teacher assessments are included in the report
☐   I have seen examples of completed reports and talked them through with an experienced colleague

Chapter 7

Critical Reflection (CR1)

The best teachers combine their talent, enthusiasm, hard work, personality and perseverance with a willingness to think about their work and make improvements on the basis of advice from others and intelligent reflection. In short, effective teachers never stop learning. This important quality is contained within a single specific statement but is implicit in many others:

CR1 Evaluating your teaching as a means of improving it.

CR1 To evaluate your own teaching critically and use this to improve your teaching effectiveness

(Section B, 4n)

What you need to take account of to meet this standard ...

Critical evaluation is not the same as destructive criticism

A critical evaluation is achieved by scrutinising your practice openly and honestly, acknowledging strengths and weaknesses, and looking to ways of improving the situation. Constant fault-finding and criticism is not likely to improve your teaching and is more likely to result in a downward spiralling level of confidence. Your first question should always be, 'Where have I succeeded?' and not 'Where did I go wrong?'. Your mentor will often give you a helpful evaluation of a particular lesson, but you can self-evaluate at any time. By using Table 15 as a guide for your self-evaluation, you will probably find that most of the points can be graded as satisfactory or better.

Keynote: To look at achievements as well as shortcomings.

No lesson is perfect

Regardless of your skill in planning, awareness of individual needs, careful resourcing, excellent presentation, appropriate task-setting and perceptive assessments,

Table 15   Critical evaluation of progress in teaching

Rate yourself on a scale of Excellent (10)/Satisfactory (5)/Weak (1)	
• Lesson preparation, including learning intentions	1................................. 10
• Availability of resources	....
• Lesson introduction	....
• Explanation of tasks and activities	....
• Monitoring of pupil behaviour and application to task	....
• Assessment of pupils' progress	....
• Ending the lesson	....
• Links with other lessons	....
• Motivating pupils	....
• Self-motivation	....
• Use of other adults (see FPT, Chapter 4)	....
• Marking and homework procedures	....

every lesson can be improved. In truth, some lessons will be outstanding, some will be dire, and the majority are likely to be satisfactory. The secret is gradually to reduce the worst and increase the best. It is often difficult to know why some lessons 'take off' and others do not. There are sometimes factors beyond your immediate control that are affecting the situation (such as the fact that there is an after-school games match causing underlying excitement). Similarly, the presence or absence of one significant pupil can change the whole class atmosphere. Persevere to improve, learn from mistakes and press forward.

Keynote: To avoid too much self-analysis.

Evaluations need to be focused

Although many teachers express satisfaction after what they perceive to have been a 'good' lesson or dismay following an 'awful' lesson, the criteria that they use to make such claims need to be more explicit, especially for student teachers. The most helpful evaluations relate to just one or two major aspects of the lesson (such as organisation or discipline) and the overall progress of the group or class (determined through written output, test results, pupils' comments, and so forth). Sometimes, a lesson seems to go well for no reason other than the children are well occupied and get on with their work. On other occasions, an apparently disastrous type of lesson can seem less terrible if learning has taken place in spite of the turmoil. A lesson can go well in terms of the settled atmosphere, but badly in terms of the pupils' progress. By contrast, a lesson in which there appears to be an excessive amount of disruptive behaviour may have much firmer learning outcomes.

Close analysis of lesson components is useful but does not give a complete picture as many elements of lesson management and organisation are closely related; failure in one area (especially preparation and class control) can result in disappointment, regardless of the effort put into others.

Keynote: To pinpoint key areas for close analysis.

Evaluations also need to take a long-term view

Your lesson may have lacked the quality and precision that you would have ideally liked, but you may have made substantial progress in building your confidence, working with other teachers, grouping children imaginatively or coping with a difficult child. Your immediate evaluation may find a number of areas for improvement, yet your long-term prospects for effective teaching may have been improved due to your willingness to tackle demanding elements of classroom life. Time spent in school has to be viewed as a whole as some days will go better than others; it is the overall improvement across a period of time that counts.

Keynote: To measure progress over both the short and long term.

The standards espouse creative teaching

Despite its formal tone and fixed requirements, Circulars 10/97 and 4/98 stress that professionalism is more than meeting a set of discrete standards but requires individual teacher's creativity, commitment, enthusiasm, intellect and management skills. When you evaluate your teaching, you need to bear in mind the extent to which your teaching conforms with these elements as well as the planning, delivery and assessment cycle. It is important not to be overwhelmed by the many demands that teaching makes and neglect your own instinct and natural ability. As an intelligent and thinking person, you will need to be familiar with the vocabulary of teaching and discuss different aspects of your work as a teacher with colleagues and fellow students. In this way you will be both a teacher of children and an adult learner. Your creativity will be stifled if you passively accept what others say about teaching without establishing your own educational values and priorities.

Keynote: To adopt a positive and thoughtful approach to teaching.

Be willing to acknowledge your weaknesses and celebrate your strengths.

Competence check

- ☐ I am spending time thinking about why I do things as well as how I do them
- ☐ I am using a structured approach in my evaluations
- ☐ I am using my evaluations and reflections to enhance my own learning

Conclusion

The demands and the large number of individual statements made by Circular 4/98 may cause you to feel that teaching is now intended to be little more than conforming to a prescribed set of procedures with little room for innovation and flair. Nothing could be further from the truth. Every school needs dedicated teachers who will use their professional judgement, knowledge, personality and determination to inspire children and enhance their learning. The Circular acknowledges that effective teaching consists of more than mere compliance with a set of criteria, however carefully expressed:

> Professionalism implies more than meeting a series of discrete standards. It is necessary to consider the standards as a whole to appreciate the creativity, commitment, energy and enthusiasm which teaching demands, and the intellectual and managerial skills required of the effective professional. (DfEE 1998, p. 8)

Four of the words from the quotation are particularly crucial to success, encouraging teachers to be:

- creative;
- committed;
- energetic;
- enthusiastic.

You will not go far wrong if these descriptors can be applied positively to you.

Finally, never lose sight of the impact that your teaching can have on the lives of the hundreds of children with whom you work. The notion that 'no one forgets a good teacher' may be a little fanciful, but it is worth holding on to.

References

Arnold, R. (1990) 'Making the best use of teacher time', in Craig, I. (ed.) *Managing the Primary Classroom*. Harlow: Longman.

Broadfoot, P. (1996) 'Do we really need to write it all down? Managing the challenge of national assessment at Key Stage 1 and Key Stage 2', in Croll, P. (ed.) *Teachers, Pupils and Primary Schooling*. London: Cassell.

Brown, G. and Wragg, E. C. (1993) *Explaining*. London: Routledge.

Clemson, D. and Clemson, W. (1996) *The Really Practical Guide to Primary Assessment*. Cheltenham: Stanley Thornes.

Cole, M. (ed.) (1999) *Professional Issues for Teachers and Student Teachers*. London: David Fulton Publishers.

Collins, J. (1996) *The Quiet Child*. London: Cassell.

Cooper, P. and McIntyre, D. (1995) *Effective Teaching and Learning: Teachers' and Pupils' Perspectives*. Buckingham: Open University Press.

DfEE (1997) *Teaching: High Status, High Standards* (Circular 10/97). London: Teacher Training Agency Publications.

DfEE (1998) *Induction for New Teachers*. Sudbury: DfEE Publications.

DfEE (1998) *Teaching: High Status, High Standards; Requirements for Courses of Initial Teacher Training* (Circular 4/98). London: Teacher Training Agency Publications.

DfEE/Welsh Office (1994) *Code of Practice on the Identification and Assessment of Special Educational Needs*. London: HMSO.

Drummond, M. J. (1993) *Assessing Children's Learning*. London: David Fulton Publishers.

Gipps, C., Brown, M. and McAlister, S. (1995) *Intuition or Evidence? Teachers and National Assessment of Seven-Year-Olds*. Buckingham: Open University Press.

Hayes, D. (1996) *Foundations of Primary Teaching*. London: David Fulton Publishers.

Hayes, D. (1998) *Effective Verbal Communication*. London: Hodder and Stoughton.

Inman, S. and Buck, M. (1995) *Adding Value? Schools' Responsibility for Pupils' Personal Development*. Stoke-on-Trent: Trentham.

Jones, K. and Charlton, T. (eds) (1996) *Overcoming Learning and Behaviour Difficulties: Partnership With Pupils*. London: Routledge.

Kyriacou, C. (1991) *Essential Teaching Skills*. Cheltenham: Stanley Thornes.

Lindsay, G. and Desforges, M. (1998) *Baseline Assessment: Practice, Problems and Possibilities*. London: David Fulton Publishers.

Littledyke, M. and Huxford, L. (1998) *Teaching the Primary Curriculum for Constructive Learning*. London: David Fulton Publishers.

McNamara, S. and Moreton, G. (1997) *Understanding Differentiation*. London: David Fulton Publishers.

Merry, R. (1998) *Successful Children, Successful Teaching*. Buckingham: Open University Press.

Mitchell, C. and Koshy, V. (1995) *Effective Teacher Assessment: Looking at Children's Learning in the Primary Classroom*, Second edn. London: Hodder and Stoughton.

Noddings, N. (1992) *The Challenge to Care in Schools: An Alternative Approach to Education*. New York: Teachers' College Press.

Office for Standards in Education/DfEE (1996) *Setting Targets to Raise Standards: A Survey of Good Practice*. London: DfEE.

Office for Standards in Education (1995) *Homework in Primary and Secondary Schools*. London: HMSO.

Pascal, C. and Bertram, T. (1997) *Effective Early Learning: Case Studies in Improvement*. London: Hodder and Stoughton.

Qualifications and Curriculum Authority (1997) *The National Framework for Baseline Assessment: Criteria and Procedures for the Accreditation of Baseline Assessment Schemes*. London: QCA.

Qualifications and Curriculum Authority (1998) *The Baseline Assessment Information Pack*. London: QCA.

SCAA (1995) *Exemplification of Standards*. Sudbury: SCAA Publications.

SCAA (1997) *Desirable Outcomes for Children's Learning on Entering Compulsory Education*. London: HMSO.

Stern, J. (1995) *Learning to Teach*. London: David Fulton Publishers.

Suschitzky, W. and Chapman, J. (1998) *Valued Children, Informed Teaching*. Buckingham: Open University Press.

Teare, B. (1997) *Effective Provision for Able and Talented Children*. Stafford: Network Educational Press.

Tymms, P. (1996) *Baseline Assessment and Value-Added: A Report to the Schools' Curriculum and Assessment Authority*. London: SCAA.

Wassermann, S. (1990) *Serious Players in the Primary Classroom: Empowering Children Through Active Learning Experiences*. New York: Teachers' College Press.

Wragg, E. C. (1994) *An Introduction to Classroom Observation*. London: Routledge.

Index